Stitching with Two-Hole Shaped Beads

VIRGINIA JENSEN

KB
KALMBACH BOOKS

Kalmbach Books
21027 Crossroads Circle
Waukesha, Wisconsin 53186
www.Kalmbach.com/Books

Published in 2015
19 18 17 16 15   2 3 4 5 6

Manufactured in the United States of America

ISBN: 978-1-62700-152-6
EISBN: 978-1-62700-153-3

Editor: Erica Swanson
Book Design: Carole Ross
Technical Editor: Jane Danley Cruz
Photographers: William Zuback and James Forbes

Library of Congress Control Number: 2014950472

Contents

Chapter 5 Herringbone

Chapter 6 Crossweave

Chapter 7 Right-Angle Weave

Chapter 8 Cluster Stitch

CLUSTER GALLERY

ACKNOWLEDGEMENTS AND ABOUT THE AUTHOR

Introduction

Two holes! What a fun concept. We all must have been ready for something new because beaders everywhere have snapped up these new two-hole beads, with their equally exciting new colors and shapes.

Of course, the stitches all have to be rewritten to accomodate the two holes, and that is what this book is about. I've brought in as many of the new shapes as I could, especially the most popular. As of the writing of this book, there are two-hole squares, bricks, Rullas, SuperDuos, twins, large and small studs, daggers, lentils, and triangles. By the time you read this, there will likely be more.

Some of the stitches in this book are derived from the usual one-hole stitches, such as herringbone, peyote, and right-angle weave. Others have evolved out of working with the beads themselves, such as the braid and cluster stitches. The examples chosen for this book are flat weave pieces; there is no three-dimensional or round work. Some two-hole beads lend themselves more to flat work than others. Other two-hole beads work better as accents or in round work. I give you my favorites, but I hope you will explore all the possibilities that call out to you.

I've started each new stitch with an easy piece and moved on to more involved designs. If you're a beginner, there should be plenty of easy pieces and basic techniques here that you can learn. New beaders can start with the early pieces in a chapter and increase their skills as the chapter continues Seasoned beaders will have fun and challenge themselves with the more difficult designs. There is something for everyone in this book.

I know some of my readers are experimenters and adventurers. Rather than just a single design, I give you options and substitutions. If you're like me, you look into the beads you already have before buying.

I hope you'll have fun with these designs. Enjoy wearing them and sharing the pieces you make with your family and friends.

— Virginia

A NOTE ABOUT ILLUSTRATIONS

This book contains companion illustrations for all of the written instructions. If you're a visual learner, these illustrations will guide you through each project, step-by-step.

Follow the order of colors: red, blue, orange, green, and then purple. The beginning of each color is indicated with a matching colored dot, showing where to start. Each new illustration starts over again with new colors.

These illustrated beads are not colored. I've found that using color in the illustrations is confusing, because what is dark for the author may be light in the reader's palette. These illustrations use shading to indicate old and new beads. The beads already incorporated are lighter and the new beads are darker. I have added a bit of color when it was useful to indicate a pattern or to draw attention to a particular bead or action.

The written instructions are keyed to the illustrations as well, so you can work them together as you choose.

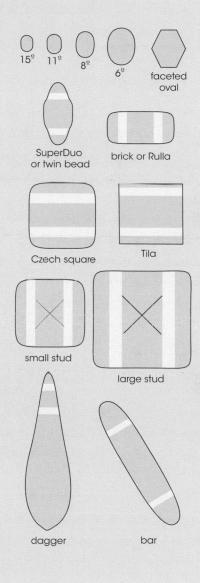

Basics

Tools

My tools have not changed substantially in over 10 years. I still love my #10 beading needles and 8- or 10-lb. test Power Pro. But I encourage beaders to work with what suits them and makes a sound and attractive piece of work.

Your **thread** should be flexible, strong, non-stretch, and, if possible, braided (so it's harder to split and catch). I use 8-lb. test Power Pro for earrings and fine work, and switch to 10-lb. for necklaces and heavy bracelets. Fireline is a good alternative.

I've tried different **needles** and will switch to #11 or #12 if needed, but I prefer the standard #10. When I use anything finer, I find myself bending them into unusable shapes. With my sturdy #10s, I just use pliers to straighten them a bit, and I'm back in business.

You'll need a place to lay out your beads, such as a **felt mat**, **sticky mat**, or **bowls**. I love my little white oriental dipping bowls. It's easier to move the beads around en masse and pick up the beads without catching the tip of the needle. They require less contortion of the hand, and when I'm finished, it's easy to pour the beads into my hand and back into their home containers.

Other necessities include **scissors** that cut cleanly and closely, a couple of **fine pliers**, a **ruler** (preferably with millimeter markings), a **magnifier** (you're bound to need it eventually), and finally, **good light**.

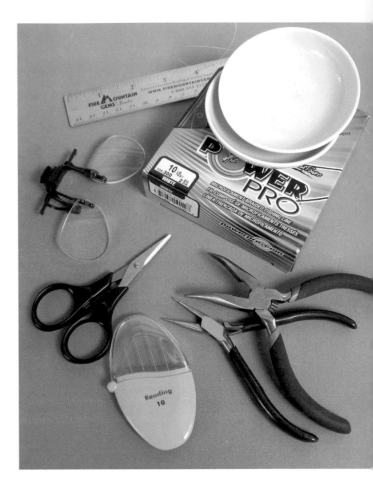

MAKE FRIENDS WITH YOUR OPHTHALMOLOGIST if you have any problem seeing your work. I've solved a couple of issues with just a lens correction or a different pair of glasses more suited to beadwork.

Two-Hole Beads

I've had so much fun working with these new beads! I believe they are here to stay. I do have my favorites, and for this book, I've stayed with the ones that work well in continuous stitches. You'll find mainly SuperDuos, bricks, Rullas, squares, and studs.

Some of the other two-hole beads have limited use for continuous stitches, but I see them in a lot of other beadwork and they look great. Some two-hole beads don't match the thickness of other beads, and two-hole triangles are very difficult to get turned the right way; however, they look great incorporated in round and three-dimensional work.

Feel free to try anything that comes into your head! I've only scratched the surface of what can be done with these beads. I hope you'll join me in exploring and creating with them.

■ Challenges with Two-Hole Beads

Clogged Holes: One of the biggest worries when working with these beads is finding one of the holes plugged after you've incorporated it into the work. After this happened to me the first, second, and third time, I started testing the holes. This usually only happens with pressed glass beads and the narrower beads, such as SuperDuos and twins, Rullas, and bricks. The condition is worse when there is a coating of some kind. I haven't had any problems with the larger beads, like squares and studs. You may want to just poke out the hole, but don't do it—you may create a very sharp break right where the thread rubs, which can cut the thread.

If you ever encounter a clogged hole and have to take apart a section of work, or worse make it over, you will understand the need to test each hole. I simply poke my needle through one of the holes, and if it goes all the way through, I go into the other hole and use it to pick up the bead.

With SuperDuos, there is an even simpler way to deal with this. Get a bead bowl that is a contrasting color (mine are white). The SuperDuos will tilt when laying and you are in position to look through the upper hole and see that it's open. Then you can just pick up the bead with the lower hole and know that both holes are open.

Please don't let this little feature deter you from using these fun and interesting beads. Nothing is perfect, and they work up so beautifully to create a look you can't get from one-hole beads.

Broken Beads: I find that Tilas like to break at the corners. Work looser than usual to prevent the Tilas from rubbing or pressing against one another when moving. (You won't have this problem with pressed glass beads.)

Size: Coating will add to the size of any bead. Sometimes manufacturers will make the beads slightly smaller to take up the difference, and sometimes they won't. When mixing colors or finishes in a piece, notice whether you have this size difference.

■ Finding Two-Hole Beads

New stores and new sellers are appearing and growing every day. Talk to your local store and ask if they will order for you. Encourage them to carry more of these new exciting two-hole beads! If you are having a hard time finding a specific bead, I've listed a few suppliers below:

> **artbeads.com:** Rullas, squares, lentils, daggers, triangles, bricks, bars, Tilas, and half-Tilas
> **fusionbeads.com:** daggers, crystals lentils, squares, bricks, triangles, 8mm and 12mm studs, Tilas, and half-Tilas
> **caravanbeads.net:** Tilas and half-Tilas
> **czechbeads.com:** squares, bricks, Rullas, daggers, SuperDuos, and lentils
> **yorkbeads.com:** 8mm and 12mm studs, 6mm tiles (squares), daggers, and 8mm piggies
> **bobbybead.com:** daggers, SuperDuos, bricks, squares, triangles, and lentils

Other Materials

Every design in this book has a materials list. The number of beads on the list are based on the actual piece associated with the design, which is usually an average size. If you want the piece to be larger or smaller, please adjust accordingly.

I assume you'll have the basic tools, and I give you the approximate amount of thread you'll need to finish the piece. Because I give you numerous options for adapting the designs, materials and quantities may change as you put together your piece. I'll offer suggestions where possible.

One of the materials you might not have on hand is 3–4mm soldered closed **jump rings**. I keep these in silver and gold color plate and use them to transition from thread to metal or wire. Don't try attaching thread to an open jump ring; the mischievous thread will invariably find the tiny gap and slip through.

With necklaces, I like to use the jump rings to end the neck strand because they let me change the clasp if I want, and I can easily add an extender when necessary. Because a bracelet is usually a smaller investment than a necklace, I attach the bracelet clasp directly to the work. I also like to minimize the clasp and show more of the beadwork—unless, of course, the clasp is a feature itself.

Techniques

My experience teaching has made me realize how important a bit of preparatory work can be when learning to bead. It's hard enough for some people to learn a stitch, and it can be much harder when they are still trying to learn how to manage thread and a needle. I may spend more time in class helping beginners untangle thread than anything else.

I've included some easy beginner pieces that are just stringing. By starting with something easy, the beginner can become familiar with the tricks thread will play on you—and they are many and varied. Take your time; you'll be glad you did later when you're able to whiz through a piece and untie the most frustrating knots.

The three areas that most puzzled me when I began beading were adding thread, tying off, and attaching clasps, so I've addressed that here.

■ Adding Thread

Just take your thread back into the work a few beads (or about a half inch), until it won't easily pull back out. Start the new thread as if running continuously from where the old thread ended, and leave a tail long enough to tie to the old thread (about 6 in./ 15cm). Work your way back to exit exactly where you were with the old thread. Your two ends are ready to tie together.

This process is much like working a maze. You may have to try several routes in your mind before finding the one that will be least visible. Practice will make this much easier. It helps if you plan this juncture to occur next to a bead that has a hole big enough to pull the knot into. I use a **surgeon's knot**, but if you have very small holes, use a square knot, as it's less bulky. After you tie the knot, take one of the ends into the nearest large hole and tug on it just a bit to get the knot to slip into the bead hole. Your knot is now hidden. Just remember not to pull so hard when finishing the other thread that you pull the knot out of the hole. Use this technique when ending the thread as well.

At first, I was eager to tie up every end and hide the tails. Now, I may just leave the tails loose until I've finished the piece, and then end everything at once. You never know what might happen before a piece is finished, and it's saved my work to have those threads untied. For example, I once noticed an error right before the changeover, and I was able to go back easily and correct it without having to laboriously pick out a knot or cut anything.

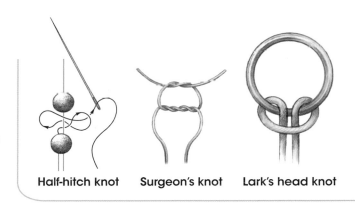

Half-hitch knot **Surgeon's knot** **Lark's head knot**

■ Ending Thread

Whenever possible I like to tie two ends together using a surgeon's knot, and then pull the knot into the nearest bead. Always run the tails away from the knot for about an inch in opposite directions before you cut them off. I've developed the habit of tying a **half-hitch knot** just a few beads before I cut. This prevents the tail from springing out.

When you have only one thread ending and must tie off, use several half-hitch knots spaced a few beads apart. Tie your half-hitch knot onto a crossing thread, if possible, so the knot will not slide forward when you move your thread on. I sometimes do a double half-hitch knot—one under a crossing thread and another under the same crossing thread, but starting in the opposite direction.

The best rule I know for working the thread through the work when adding or ending thread is this: You can go anywhere with the thread that you've already been without it showing, but if you start adding new tracks, they are more likely to show.

Don't end a thread at the edge of the work because it will be more visible. Bury it in the middle of the work and on the underside, if there is one. Pull on the end to take up any slack right before you cut it off.

■ Attaching Clasps

Plan the clasp you are going to use when you start your piece, and you will save yourself a lot of trouble. Some of the pieces in this book start with a doubled thread, so you can simply attach the loop to one end of a clasp using a **lark's head knot,** and you're done with that end.

I've used ready-made clasps in this book, because my main focus is on the stitches. But you can experiment with decorative clasps, if you like.

I like toggle clasps for narrow bracelets. When using a toggle, there must be room for the bar to fold back and enter the loop, so add a few beads to equal the length of one of the arms of the bar before attaching it. If the bracelet is very narrow or it

naturally comes to a point, you will need fewer additional beads.

Sewing on a multiple-ring clasp requires planning. You can sew the ring into a bead, onto a bead, or to the thread running between beads. To sew the ring into a bead, exit the bead through the ring and sew back into the bead. Turn around in the work, and repeat. To sew the ring to the thread between the beads, exit one side of the bead through the ring and sew back into the bead. Then sew through the other side of the bead and the ring, and sew back in.

When sewing the ring to the thread, I like to reinforce that thread by adding passes so I'm sewing onto a few threads, not just one.

With multiple rings (and depending on the stitch), you might have to use any or all of these options. Set the clasp against the end of the bracelet and study the fit. This determines which attachment will work best on each of the rings and allow the clasp to lay properly.

Remember that you can add one or more beads to extend the attachment so the clasp sits evenly across the width of the bracelet.

Never leave an attachment hanging by a single thread. I try to make two passes at the very least—and preferably three or four. This is the part of the piece that will get the most stress as the wearer puts the piece on and off.

NOW YOU'RE READY, SO LET'S BEAD! Remember to relax, stop, and stretch, or walk around every now and then. Most importantly: Have fun!

Chapter 1
Stringing

Simple, little strung bracelets are great for teaching beginners and for using up those small bags of leftover beads. Once you get the hang of working these up, you'll be inventing your own designs in no time. The technique is easy, but the pieces in this chapter will give beginners an opportunity to become familiar with some of the basics of beadwork. Learn how to attach a clasp, tie knots, manage your thread with good tension, and end your work neatly. There's no adding thread or complicated stitching; just follow the instructions and have fun.

The bracelets in this chapter start with a doubled thread. Just attach the loop of thread to the loop end of a toggle clasp using a lark's head knot, and jump right into the pattern. When you finish, attach the bar end of the clasp. Remember to add a few beads to give the bar room to bend back and enter the loop part of the clasp.

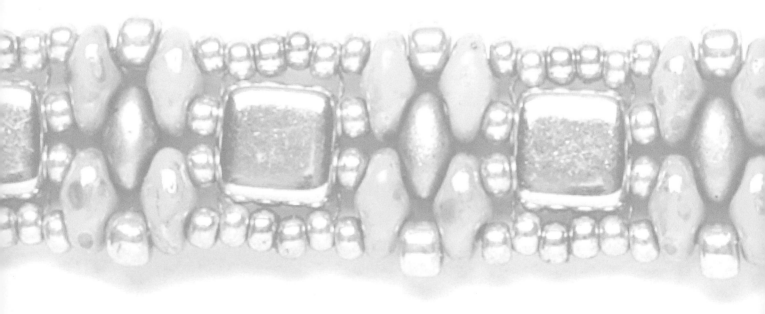

Square and Brick Bracelet

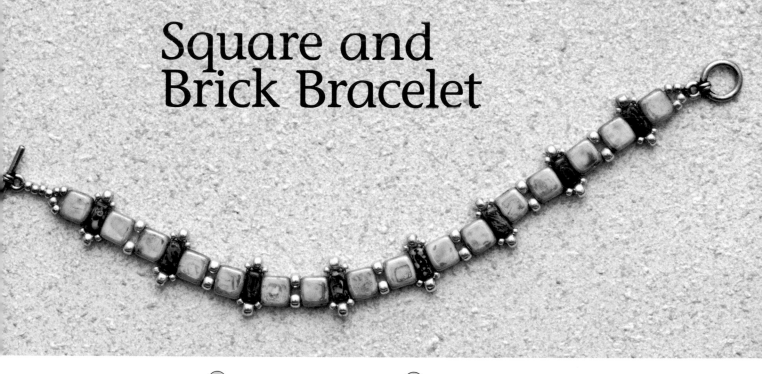

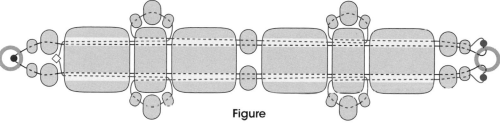

Figure

Step 1

Fold 1 yd. (.9m) of thread in half and attach the loop to one end of a clasp with a lark's head knot. Thread a needle on each end.

Step 2

[Figure, red thread] With either needle, pick up an 11º seed bead and an 8º seed bead. Pick up a square, a brick, a square, and an 8º, and repeat until you reach the desired length, ending with a square. Pick up an 8º and an 11º, and attach a stop bead to keep this side together while you work the other side. Repeat this step with the other needle, sewing through the other holes of the two-hole beads.

Step 3

[Figure, blue thread] With either needle, attach the thread to the other end of the clasp, adding beads to allow the bar to fold back, if necessary. Sew back through the 11º and 8º you exited before the clasp, and sew on back through the square and brick. * Pick up an 11º, an 8º, and an 11º, and sew through the same hole of the brick again in the same direction, taking out the slack and pulling the group of three up against the top of the brick. Continue through the next square, 8º, and brick. Repeat from the asterisk until you reach the end of the bracelet. Repeat on the other side. End the threads.

MATERIALS

6 in. (15cm) bracelet

16 squares

8 bricks

30 8º seed beads

44 11º seed beads

toggle clasp

1 yd. (.9m) thread

: OPTIONS

Try this bracelet with bricks and studs or with Tilas and half-Tilas.

Square and SuperDuo Bracelet

Step 1

Fold 1 yd. (.9m) of thread in half, and attach to one end of a clasp using a lark's head knot. Thread a needle on each end.

Step 2

[Figure, red thread] With either needle, pick up two 11º seed beads. Pick up a square, a 15º seed bead, a SuperDuo, and a 15º, and repeat until you reach the desired length, ending with a square. Pick up two 11ºs, and attach a stop bead to keep this side together while you work the other side. Repeat this step with the other needle, sewing through the other holes of the two-hole square.

Step 3

[Figure, blue thread] Remove the stop bead on either thread, and attach the thread to the other end of the clasp, adding beads to allow the bar to fold back, if necessary. Sew back through the two 11ºs, the same hole of the square you exited before the clasp, the 15º, and the same hole of the SuperDuo. * Pick up a 15º, an 11º, and a 15º. Sew through the same hole of the SuperDuo again in the same direction. Continue through the 15º, square, 15º, and SuperDuo. Repeat from the asterisk until you reach the end of the bracelet. Repeat with the other thread. End the threads.

: OPTIONS

Try this bracelet with two bricks, two Rullas, a stud, or a Tila in place of each square. You can also substitute twin beads for the SuperDuos.

MATERIALS

6 in. (15cm) bracelet

13 squares

12 SuperDuos

96 15º seed beads

32 11º seed beads

toggle clasp

1 yd. (.9m) thread

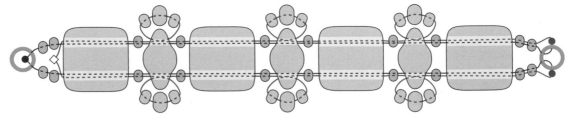

Figure

Brick Bracelet

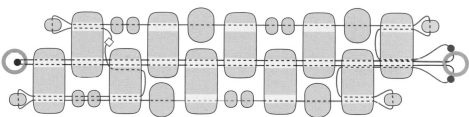

Figure

Step 1

Fold 1¼ yd. (1.14m) of thread in half, and attach to one end of a clasp using a lark's head knot. Thread both threads onto one needle.

Step 2

[Figure, red thread] Pick up all 50 bricks, and attach the other end of the clasp, remembering to add an 11º seed bead or two to allow the bar to fold back. Remove one of the threads from the needle, and thread it onto its own needle.

Step 3

[Figure, upper blue thread] With either needle, sew back through the same hole of the nearest brick. Turn and sew in the opposite direction through the

open hole of the same brick. Pick up an 11º, and sew back through the same hole of the brick. Pick up a 6º seed bead, and continue through the open hole of the third brick from the end. Pick up two 11ºs, and continue through the open hole of the fifth brick from the end. Continue alternating 6ºs and two 11ºs with every odd-numbered brick. When you have sewn through every brick you can, pick up an 11º, and sew back through the same hole of the last brick in the opposite direction. Add a stop bead here.

Step 4

[Figure, lower blue thread] With the other needle, work as in step 3, sewing through the open holes of the even-numbered bricks. End the thread.

MATERIALS

6½ in. (16.5cm) bracelet

50 bricks

24 6º seed beads

57 11º seed beads

toggle clasp

1¼ yd. (1.14m) thread

: OPTIONS

Replace the bricks with Rullas or half-Tilas.

Square with SuperDuo Ruffle Bracelet

Step 1

Fold 2 yd. (1.8m) of thread in half. Attach to one half of a clasp using a lark's head knot. Thread a needle on each end.

Step 2

[Figure 1, red thread] With either needle, pick up an 11º seed bead. * Pick up a square, an 11º, a SuperDuo, and an 11º, and repeat from the asterisk until you reach the desired length, ending with a square and 11º. Attach a stop bead while you work the other side. Repeat this step with the other needle, sewing through the open holes of the two-hole beads.

Step 3

[Figure 1, blue thread] With either needle, remove the stop bead. Remembering to add extender beads, attach the other end of the clasp, and sew back through the 11º. * Pick up a 15º seed bead, three SuperDuos, and a 15º. Sew again through the next 11º, SuperDuo, 11º group added in the previous step. Repeat from the asterisk until you reach the end of the bracelet, stopping just short of the end 11º. Sew through the nearest hole of the first square in the opposite direction. Sew through the other hole of the same square and the nearest 15º. Repeat with the other needle.

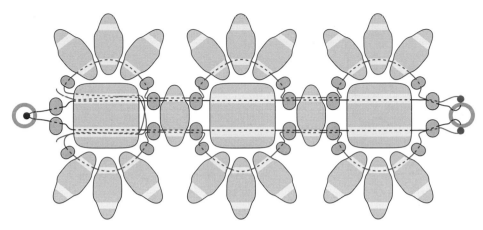

Figure 1

Figure 2

Step 4

[Figure 2, red thread] With either needle, sew through the 15º that is adjacent to the SuperDuo. Pick up two 15ºs. Sew through the open hole of the first of the three SuperDuos. * Pick up an 11º. Sew through the empty hole of the next SuperDuo, and pick up an 11º. Sew through the empty hole of the third SuperDuo. Pick up an 8º seed bead, and sew through the nearest hole of the SuperDuo between the two

squares, sewing back through the 8º and the first SuperDuo. Pull the thread and beads taut so the 8º abuts the tip of the SuperDuo below it. Repeat from the asterisk until you sew through the last group of three SuperDuos. Pick up two 15ºs, sew through the 15º at the base of the last grouping, and then sew through the last square. Repeat this step with the other needle. End the thread.

MATERIALS

6¾ in. (17.1cm) bracelet

15 squares
104 SuperDuos
28 8º seed beads
1.5g 11º seed beads
.5g 15º seed beads
toggle clasp
2 yd. (1.8m) thread

: OPTIONS
Try replacing the squares with Tilas, small studs, two bricks, or two Rullas.

Square with SuperDuo Sections Bracelet

Step 1

Fold 1½ yd. (1.4m) of thread in half and attach the loop to one end of a clasp using a lark's head knot. Thread a needle on each end.

Step 2

[Figure, red thread] With either needle, pick up two 11º seed beads, a square, an 11º, three SuperDuos, and an 11º. Repeat this pattern until you reach the desired length, ending with a square. Pick up two 11ºs, and attach a stop bead while you work the other side. Repeat this step with the other needle, sewing through the open holes of the squares, the 11ºs, and the middle SuperDuo. Pick up new SuperDuos on either side of the middle SuperDuo.

: OPTIONS

Try this bracelet with studs, two bricks, or two Rullas in place of each square.

Step 3

[Figure, blue thread] With either needle, remove the stop bead, attach the other half of the clasp, adding an 11º (or two) to allow the bar to fold back, and sew back through the two 11ºs. Pick up four 11ºs, sew back through the nearest hole of the next square with the needle pointing toward the clasp just picked up. Retrace the thread path through the four 11ºs, attaching the four 11ºs securely to the square. * Pick up an 11º, sew through the open hole of the first SuperDuo, pick up an 8º seed bead, and sew through the open hole of the third SuperDuo. Pick up five 11ºs, and sew through the square in the opposite direction and retrace the thread path. through the last four 11ºs. Repeat from the asterisk until you reach the end of the bracelet. Sew back into the first square. Repeat with the other thread. End the thread.

MATERIALS

6½ in. (16.5cm) bracelet

10 squares

45 SuperDuos

18 8º seed beads

1–2g 11º seed beads

toggle clasp

1½ yd. (1.4m) thread

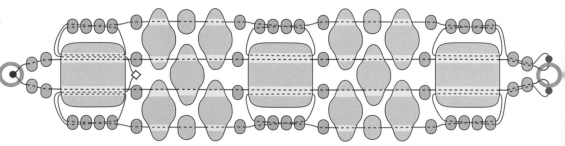

Figure

Chapter 2
Peyote Stitch

Peyote stitch is easy with SuperDuos, as they are shaped to fit tightly together. Any design you can do in peyote stitch with seed beads, you can do with SuperDuos. Straight peyote makes a sleek, snakey look and feel. For the best effect, use a glossy finish.

As with peyote stitch with one-hole beads, there is a difference in working the odd and even bead widths. In this chapter, I will show you how to do both. For the more adventurous beaders, I've included a variation on peyote stitch using squares and 1.5mm cubes that makes a gorgeous cuff—and a diagonal variation that is a blend of peyote and square stitches.

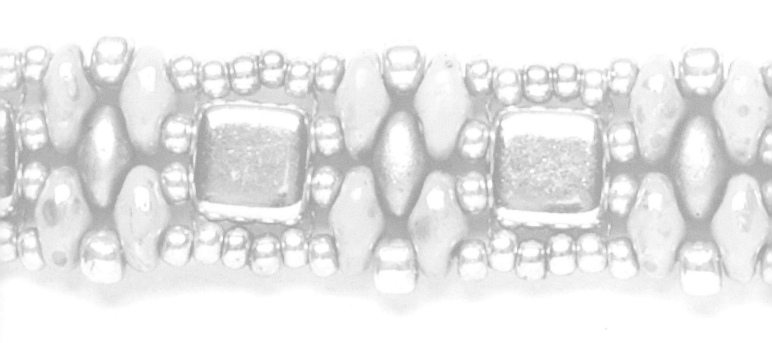

Basic Peyote Bracelet with SuperDuos

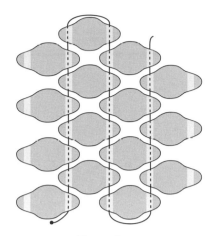

Figure 1

EVEN-COUNT PEYOTE

This is even-count peyote, which is the easiest type of peyote stitch. If you like the slinky feel and lizard-skin look, the 14-bead wide bracelet shown in the photo is for you. (For space considerations, my illustration and instructions show a bracelet that is only eight beads wide.)

Step 1

[Figure 1] Attach a stop bead or a bead stopper, and thread a needle on a comfortable length of thread, leaving a 6-in. (15cm) tail. Pick up eight Super-Duos. Turn and sew through the open hole of the last SuperDuo. Snug up the beads. * Pick up a SuperDuo, skip the next SuperDuo, and sew through the open hole of the following SuperDuo. Repeat from the asterisk twice. Pick up a SuperDuo, and sew through the open hole of the SuperDuo you just exited. Snug up the beads. Repeat from the asterisk until you reach the desired length.

Step 2

Attach a clasp half by sew through the beadwork and exiting a SuperDuo near the end. Pick up a loop on the clasp, and sew through the SuperDuo in the opposite direction. Repeat to attach the remaining loops, and repeat on the other end of the bracelet to attach the other clasp half.

MATERIALS

7¼ in. (18.4cm) band

380 SuperDuos

4-loop bar clasp to fit width

2½ yd. (2.3m) thread

: OPTIONS

Try replacing the turn-around SuperDuo at the end with a group of 15º/11º/15º or 11º/8º/11º for a different edge.

Peyote Cuff with Squares and Cubes

Step 1

[Figure 1] Thread a needle on a comfortable length of thread and attach a stop bead, leaving a 10-in. (25cm) tail. Pick up a square and six cubes. Sew back through the first three cubes in the same direction, and pull the beads together so they line up as shown in the illustration. Repeat twice, using an accent color in the middle, but on the last pass, cross over and sew through the fourth cube you picked up, instead of the third.

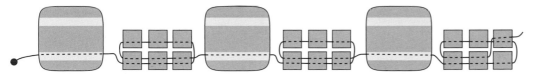

Figure 1

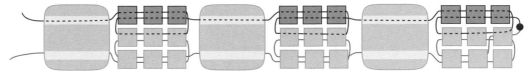

Figure 2

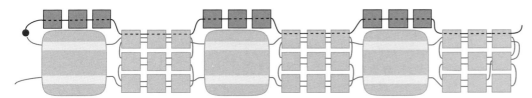

Figure 3

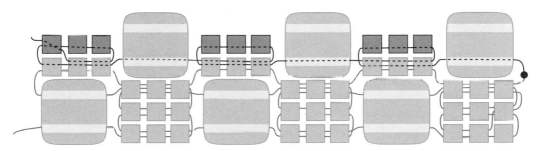

Figure 4

Step 2

[Figure 2] Pick up three cubes, turn, and sew back through the second row of cubes you added in step 1. Turn again, and sew through the three new cubes with the needle pointing toward the tail. Sew through the open hole of the square. Repeat this step twice.

Step 3

[Figure 3] Pick up three cubes, and sew through the three cubes added in the previous step. Repeat this step twice to complete the row.

Step 4

[Figure 4] Pick up a square, sew through the three cubes in the previous row. Pick up three cubes, and sew back through the three cubes in the previous row. Pull taut, and help the beads to lie securely in place before you move on. Repeat to complete the row, shifting over to the new row on the last cube as in step 1. Repeat steps 2, 3, and 4 until you reach the desired length. Sew on the clasp.

Note: Turning the work is not a simple back-and-forth motion as in one-hole peyote. Try to find the hand positions that suit you, and turn as needed.

MATERIALS

7¼ in. (18.4cm) bracelet

84 squares

8g 1.5mm cubes (1g in an accent color)

5-loop slide clasp

6 yd. (5.6m) thread

: OPTIONS

This bracelet will work up nicely with Tila beads as well as the squares.

Diagonal
Peyote Cuff
with Squares
and Cubes

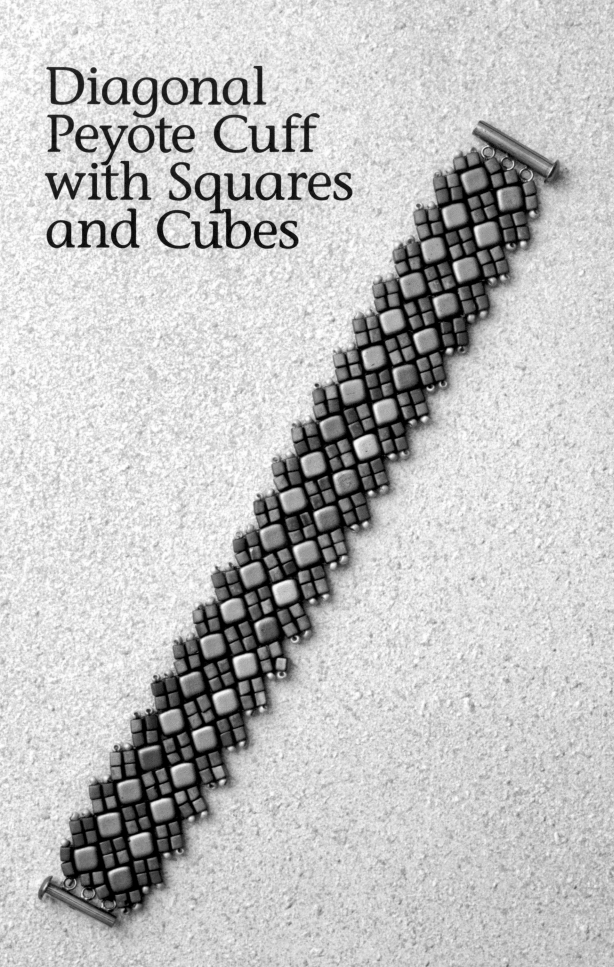

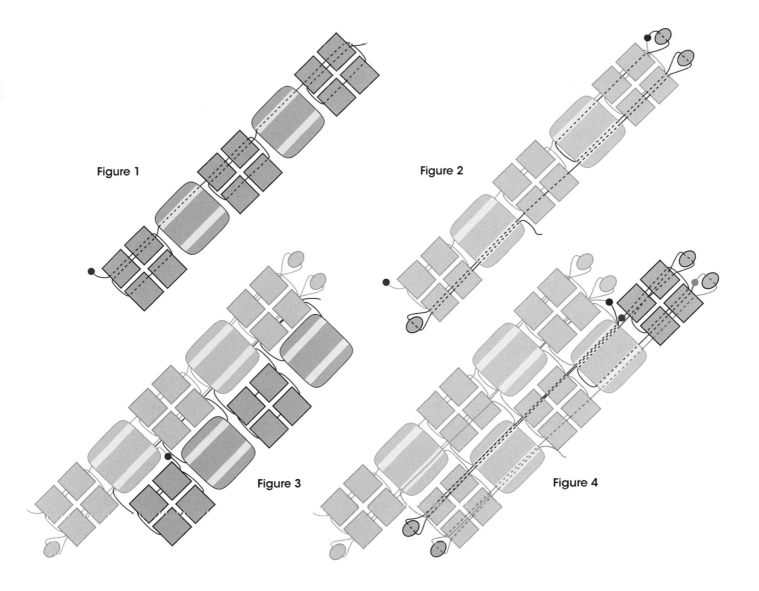

Figure 1

Figure 2

Figure 3

Figure 4

ANGLED PEYOTE

This stitch is based somewhat on the previous peyote variation, but turned at an angle. I found it easier to build the diagonal rows first and go back and fill in the triangular end sections.

Step 1

[Figure 1] Thread a needle on 3 yd. (2.7m) of thread. Add a stop bead, leaving a 1-yd. (.9m) tail; you will need this to finish the end. Pick up four cubes, sew through the first and second cubes again, and pull tight to make a box of four cubes. Pick up a square and four cubes, and make another box of four.

Pick up a square and four cubes and make a third box.

Step 2

[Figure 2] Pick up an 11º seed bead, and sew down through the two nearest cubes and the last square. Turn, and sew through the open hole of the square and following two cubes. Pick up an 11º, turn, and sew back through all of the beads on this side. Be sure to catch every bead. Pick up an 11º, turn, and sew back through the two cubes and the next square. You are now in position to start a new row.

MATERIALS

7 in. (18cm) bracelet

38 squares

242 3mm cubes

1g 11º seed beads

3-strand slide clasp

6 yd. (5.6m) thread

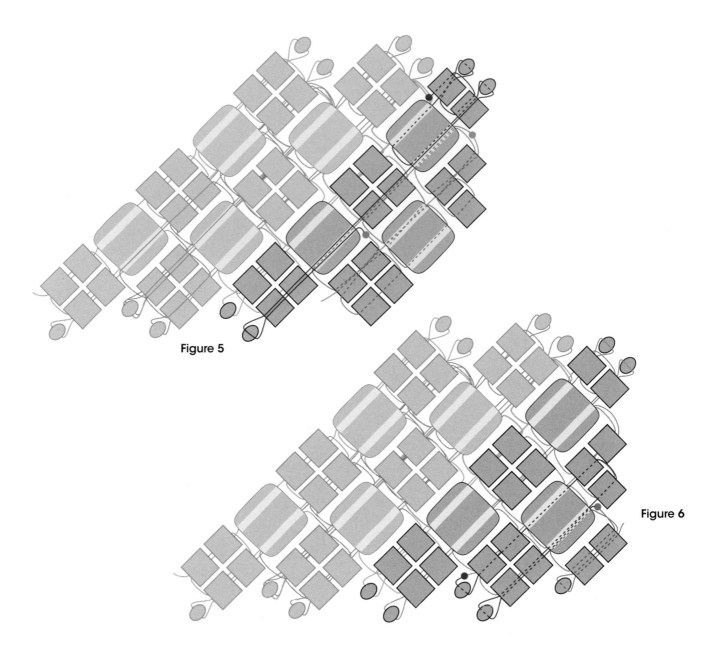

Figure 5

Figure 6

Step 3

[Figure 3] To create the pattern, pick up four cubes, and make a box. Attach the box to the adjacent square in the previous row by sewing through the nearest hole in the square, and then continuing through the next two cubes in the same row. Pick up a square, and sew through the adjacent two cubes again. Repeat, attaching another box and square.

Step 4

[Figure 4, red thread] Turn, and sew down through the square, two cubes, square, and two cubes, with the needle pointing toward the tail. Pick up an 11º, and sew back through all the beads in this row.

Step 5

[Figure 4, blue thread] Make a new box of four cubes and pull it tight against the square. Pick up an 11º, and sew back through the two cubes and the square below,

turn, and sew through the open hole of the square and the two cubes on the other side of the box.

Step 6

[Figure 4, orange thread] Pick up an 11º, and sew back through the two cubes, the square, and the remaining beads along this edge. Pick up an 11º, and sew back through the two cubes and the first square. You are ready to start another row.

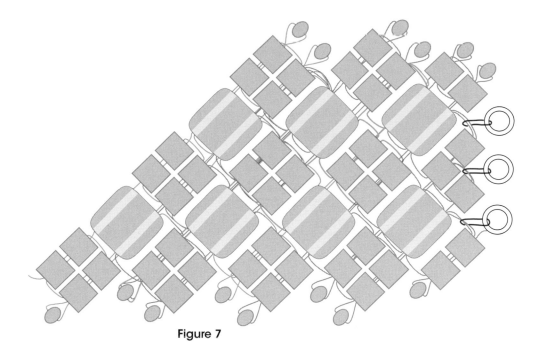

Figure 7

Step 7

Repeat steps 3–6 for the desired length.

Step 8

[Figure 5, red thread] To finish the ends, add a final row and build a half-box at the end by picking up two cubes and sewing back through the first cube. Pick up an 11º, and sew back through the cube and the square. Turn, and sew through the open hole of the square and the end cube. Pick up an 11º, and sew back through all the beads on the edge. Pick up an 11º, and sew up through the two cubes and the square.

Step 9

[Figure 5, blue thread] Attach the box of four cubes and the square as usual, and continue up through the next square in the previous row.

Step 10

[Figure 5, orange thread] Instead of picking up a box of four, pick up two cubes and attach them to the square in the previous row. Exit the two new cubes with the needle pointing toward the tail. Attach a third cube to the bottom cube, and continue through the square and two cubes.

Step 11

[Figure 6, red thread] Pick up an 11º and sew back through two cubes, the square, and a cube. Turn, and sew down through the adjacent cube, the square, and two cubes. Pick up an 11º, turn, and sew back up through the two cubes and the square.

Step 12

[Figure 6, blue thread] Attach two cubes to the square, as before.

Pick up an 11º, turn, and sew back through the two cubes.

Step 13

Finish the other end by reversing the piece so it looks just like the first end. Pick up an 11º, bring the thread to the point between the first square and the second box, and make another row, ending with a half cube.

Note: You will have to allow for this additional row in planning for the final length.

Continue as in steps 8–11 to finish the bracelet.

Step 14

[Figure 7, red thread] Attach a clasp by sewing the rings to the double threads as shown in the illustration. End the thread. Repeat for the other end of the bracelet.

Chapter 3
braid stitch

Braid is a stitch developed especially for two-hole beads. I love the simple, classic look of the basic pieces, done here using Rullas and SuperDuos. I also show you how to adapt it to work with bricks, squares, and bars, as well as how to help the double braid band curve into a beautiful necklace.

This is a versatile stitch, which can be adapted to work with many different sizes and shapes of two-hole beads. I was excited each time I tried it with a new two-hole bead—it always rewarded me with a great look. I hope you'll explore some of the other possibilities as new two-hole beads become available.

Tension is very important in braid stitch. If you don't keep constant tension on the thread, you will have large gaps along the sides. Here's how I do it. After you finish step 1 of any of the following projects, wrap the thread around your middle finger and press your index finger against the thread to lock it in place. Pick up the two edging seed beads, and sew through the open upper hole of the bead you just exited. Pull through, but don't let go of the tension—the thread will still be wrapped around your finger. Pick up the next beads, and sew down through the lower hole of the last bead on the other side. Pull through. Release the thread wrapped around your finger, and quickly draw out all the slack. Turn the work. Wrap the thread immediately around your finger again. You are ready to repeat.

S-Braid Bracelet with SuperDuos

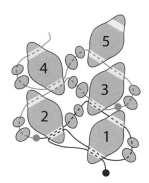

Figure

Step 1

[Figure, red thread] Thread a needle on a comfortable length of thread, and pick up two SuperDuos. Turn, and sew through the same hole of the first SuperDuo in the opposite direction. Butt the tip of the second bead against the hole of the first bead, and hold these two beads in place until you get a few more beads added. Pick up an 11º seed bead and a 15º seed bead. Turn, and sew through the open hole of the first SuperDuo. Pick up a SuperDuo, a 15º, and an 11º, and sew through the first hole of the second SuperDuo. Pull tight, and turn the work.

Step 2

[Figure, blue thread] This begins the pattern: Pick up an 11º and a 15º, and sew through the open hole of the SuperDuo you just exited. Pick up a SuperDuo, a 15º, and an 11º, and sew through the first hole of the last SuperDuo on the other side.

Step 3

[Figure, orange thread] Turn, and repeat step 2 for the desired length.

Step 4

This stitch creatres an uneven end, so you will need to add 15ºs or 11ºs to fill the space needed to attach the clasp (see photo). Attach the clasp, and end the threads.

MATERIALS

8 in. (20cm) bracelet

84 SuperDuos

1.5g 11º seed beads

1g 15º seed beads

toggle clasp

2 yd. (1.8m) thread

: OPTION

You can use two 15ºs instead of an 11º and a 15º— or whatever seed bead combination will fit.

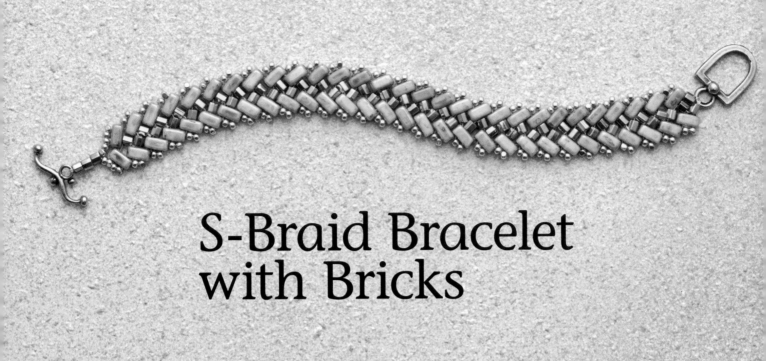

S-Braid Bracelet with Bricks

Step 1

[Figure, red thread] Thread a needle on a comfortable length of thread, and pick up two bricks and two 15º seed beads. Turn and sew through the open hole of the second brick. Pick up a third brick and a square. Sew down through the lower hole of the first brick you picked up. Turn the work.

Step 2

[Figure, blue thread] Pick up two 15ºs, turn, and sew through the open hole of the first bead. Pick up a fourth brick and a square. Sew through the lower hole of the third brick. Turn the work.

: OPTIONS

I've used 4mm Czech cubes between the bricks in my designs. Their rounded corners and shape match the bricks best. But you can use any bead that will fit, such as 8º seed beads, small faceted rounds or ovals, or glass or stone rounds.

Step 3

[Figure, orange thread] To begin the pattern: Pick up two 15ºs, turn, and sew through the open hole of the bead you just exited. Pick up a new brick and a square, and sew through the lower hole of the last brick on the other side. Turn the work. Repeat step 3 until you reach the desired length. Add 8º seed beads or 15ºs to fill the space needed to attach the clasp (see photo). Attach the clasp, and end the threads.

MATERIALS

7 in. (18cm) bracelet

56 bricks

28 4mm Czech cubes or 8º seed beads

1g 15º seed beads

toggle clasp

2 yd. (1.9m) thread

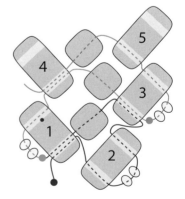

Figure

S-Braid Bracelet with Squares

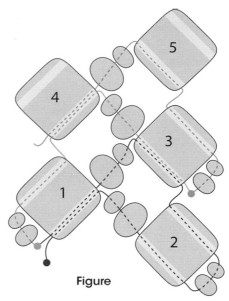

Figure

Step 1

[Figure, red thread] Thread a needle on a comfortable length of thread, and pick up a square, an 8º seed bead, a 6º seed bead, and a square. Pick up an 8º and an 11º seed bead, turn, and sew through the open hole of the second square. Pick up a third square, an 8º, and a 6º, and sew through the lower hole of the first square you picked up. Turn the work.

Step 2

[Figure, blue thread] Pick up an 8º and an 11º, turn, and sew through the open hole of the first bead. Pick up a fourth square, an 8º, and a 6º. Sew through the lower hole of the third square. Turn the work.

Step 3

[Figure, orange thread] Pick up an 8º and an 11º, turn, and sew through the open hole of the bead you just exited. Pick up a new square, an 8º, and a 6º. Sew down through the lower hole of the last square on the other side of the bracelet. Turn the work. Repeat step 3 until you reach the desired length. Add 6ºs, 8ºs, or 15º seed beads to fill the space needed to attach the clasp (see photo). Attach the clasp, and end the threads.

MATERIALS

7 in. (18cm) bracelet

44 squares

4g 6º seed beads

2g 8º seed beads

.5g 11º seed beads

toggle clasp

2 yd. (1.8m) thread

S-Braid with Two-Hole Bars

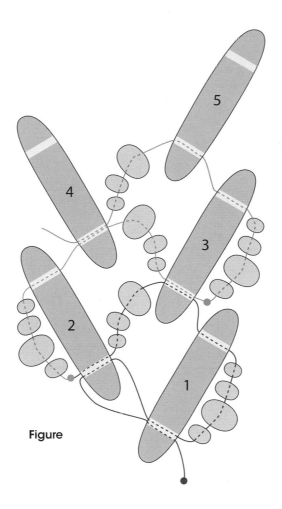

Figure

Step 1

[Figure, red thread] Thread a needle on a comfortable length of thread, and pick up two two-hole bars. Turn, and sew through the first bar in the same hole in the opposite direction. Butt the tip of the second bead against the hole of the first bead, and hold these two beads in place until you get a few more beads added. Pick up an 8º, a 6º, an 8º, and an 11º seed bead, turn, and sew through the open hole of the second bar. Pick up a third bar, a 6º, an 8º, and an 11º, and sew through the lower hole of the second bar. Turn the work.

Step 2

[Figure, blue thread] Pick up an 8º, a 6º, an 8º, and an 11º. Turn, and sew through the open hole of the first bar. Pick up a fourth bar, a 6º, an 8º, and an 11º, and sew through the lower hole of the third bar. Turn the work.

Step 3

[Figure, orange thread] Pick up an 8º, a 6º, an 8º, and an 11º, turn, and sew through the open hole of the bead you just exited. Pick up a new bar, a 6º, an 8º, and an 11º. Sew through the lower hole of the last square on the other side of the bracelet. Turn the work. Repeat step 3 until you reach the desired length. Add 8ºs or 15º seed beads to fill the space needed to attach the clasp (see photo). Attach the clasp. End the threads.

MATERIALS

7½ in. (19.1cm) bracelet

28 two-hole bars

32 6º seed beads

2g 8º seed beads

1g 11º seed beads

toggle clasp

2 yd. (1.8m) thread

Double Braid
Bracelet with
Rullas

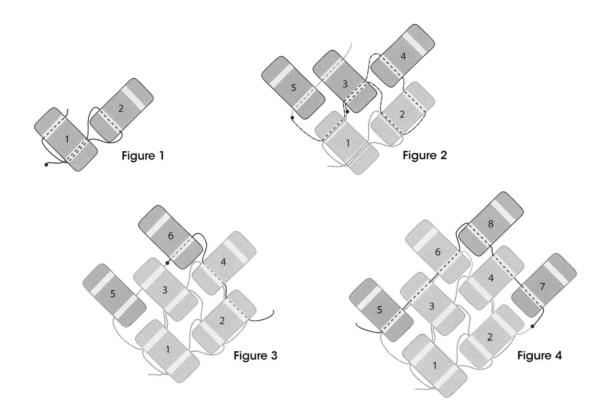

Figure 1

Figure 2

Figure 3

Figure 4

Step 1

[Figure 1] Thread a needle on a comfortable length of thread, and pick up two color A Rullas (1 and 2). Turn and sew down through the same hole of the first Rulla in the opposite direction. Turn and sew up through the other hole of the A.

Step 2

[Figure 2, red thread] Pick up an A (3). Sew down through the lower hole of the second Rulla. Turn and sew up through the upper hole of the same Rulla. Pick up an A (4). Sew down through the lower hole of the third Rulla and on down through the upper hole of the first Rulla. **[blue thread]** Pick up a color B

Rulla (5), and sew up through the upper hole of the third Rulla.

Step 3

[Figure 3] Pick up an A (6). Turn and sew down through the lower hole of the fourth Rulla, and continue down through the upper hole of the second Rulla.

Step 4

[Figure 4] Pick up a B (7), and sew up through the upper hole of the fourth Rulla. Pick up an A. Turn and sew down through the lower hole of the sixth Rulla, the upper hole of the third Rulla, and the lower hole of the fifth Rulla. Turn the work over.

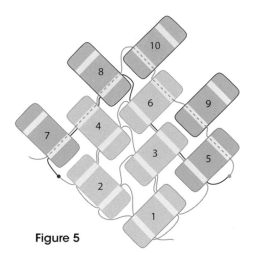

Figure 5

Step 5

[Figure 5, red thread] This thread shows how the last thread looks when turned. You will be turning regularly to make the stitching easier. I like to sew down through the three Rullas, wrap the thread around my finger to hold the tension, turn, and start the next step.

Step 6

[Figure 5, blue thread] Sew through the upper hole of the fifth Rulla. Pick up a B (9), and continue through the upper hole of the sixth Rulla. Pick up an A (10). Turn and sew down through the lower hole of the eighth Rulla, the upper hole of the fourth Rulla, and the lower hole of the seventh Rulla. Turn the work.

Step 7

Step 6 establishes the pattern. Always start by turning and sewing up through the upper hole of the right-most Rulla, picking up a B, and continuing on through the upper hole of the next Rulla. Then pick up an A and sew down through the three Rullas on the left, lower, upper, then lower holes. You are in position to turn and repeat.

Step 8

When you reach the desired length, add a clasp half to each end by sewing through an end Rulla and picking up an 8º seed bead (if needed) and one loop of the clasp. Sew back through the beads, and continue through the beadwork to exit the other end Rulla to add the second loop. Repeat on the other end of the bracelet.

: OPTIONS
Try this double braid with bricks or half-Tilas.

Double Braid
Necklace
with Rullas
and
SuperDuos

Figure

[Figure] Refer to the "Double Braid Bracelet with Rullas," p. 38, and make a curved braid: Work the lower edge the same as the upper edge, except change the small beads to make the piece curve. Along the lower edge, add an 11º seed bead instead of a 15º seed bead between the two SuperDuos every other time **[yellow bead]**.

Along the upper edge, leave out the 15º between the SuperDuos altogether **[red X]**. This small change allows the piece to curve nicely into a necklace. Sew a soldered jump ring to each end. Use open 3mm jump rings to attach a clasp to one end and the chain to the other end.

MATERIALS

17 in. (43cm) necklace

188 Rullas

164 SuperDuos

.5g 11º seed beads

1g 15º seed beads

2 in. (5cm) chain

2 3mm soldered
   jump rings

2 3mm open jump rings

lobster claw clasp

6 yd. (5.6m) thread

Double Braid Bracelet with Bricks and Squares

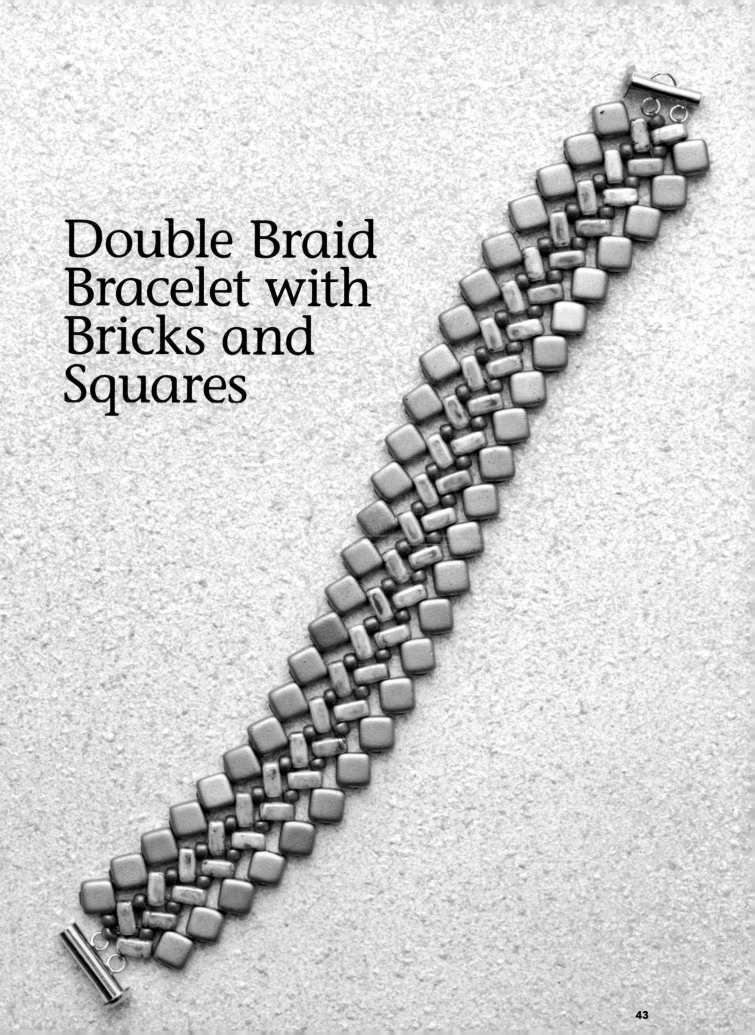

Figure 1

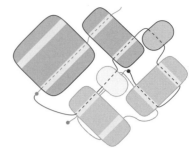

Figure 2

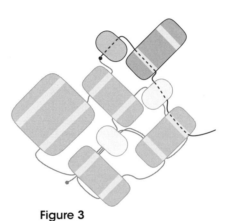

Figure 3

: OPTIONS

Add a couple of seed beads to decorate the edge when you turn to sew up the outside in Figure 5. To make a Tila version, replace the squares with Tilas and the bricks with half-Tilas.

Step 1

[Figure 1] Thread a needle on 2 yd. (1.8m) of thread. Leaving an 8-in. (20cm) tail, pick up a brick, an 8º seed bead, and a brick. Sew through the second hole of the first brick in the opposite direction, sew back through the first hole of the first brick, and continue through the 8º.

Step 2

[Figure 2, red thread] Sew down through the same hole of the second brick, and then sew through the open hole of the same brick. Pick up an 8º and a brick. Sew down through the previous 8º and brick. **[blue thread]** Pick up a square, and sew through the open hole of the previous brick.

Step 3

[Figure 3] Pick up an 8º and a brick. Sew through the previous 8º and the nearest hole of the second brick.

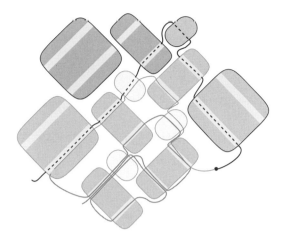

Figure 4

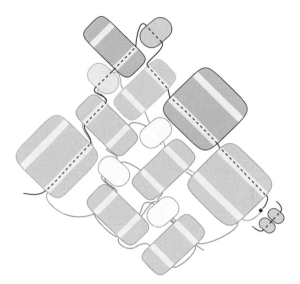

Figure 5

Step 4

[Figure 4] Pick up a square, and sew through the open hole of the last brick added in the previous step. Pick up an 8º and a brick. Sew back through the 8º, brick, and adjacent square.

Step 5

[Figure 5] Turn the work from left to right. Sew through the open hole of the square your thread is exiting, pick up a square, and continue up through the open hole of the next brick. Pick up an 8º and a brick. Turn and sew through the 8º added in the previous step, the nearest hole of the brick, and the lower hole of the square. This establishes the pattern. Turn the work and repeat until you reach the desired length.

Step 6

Add 6º, 8º, or 15º seed beads to fill the space needed to attach the clasp (see photo). Attach the clasp, and end the threads.

MATERIALS

7 in. (18cm) bracelet

48 bricks

48 squares or Tilas

1.5g 8º seed beads

2-loop slide clasp

4 yd. (3.7m) thread

Chapter 4
step stitch

Step stitch is a stitch developed from St. Petersburg chain. Since the stitch is now more than just a chain, I adopted its Russian name, which translates as "stair" or "step" stitch. As you'll see, step stitch is based on the building of little "boxes" of beads, whether it's two bricks or four cubes.

I start with a simple version that has a contemporary look. The more complex the patterns become, the more option there is for variation. I use color, shape, and texture to create interesting patterns within each piece. If you find this stitch interesting, you'll find much more of it in my second book, *Contemporary Cube Bead Designs*.

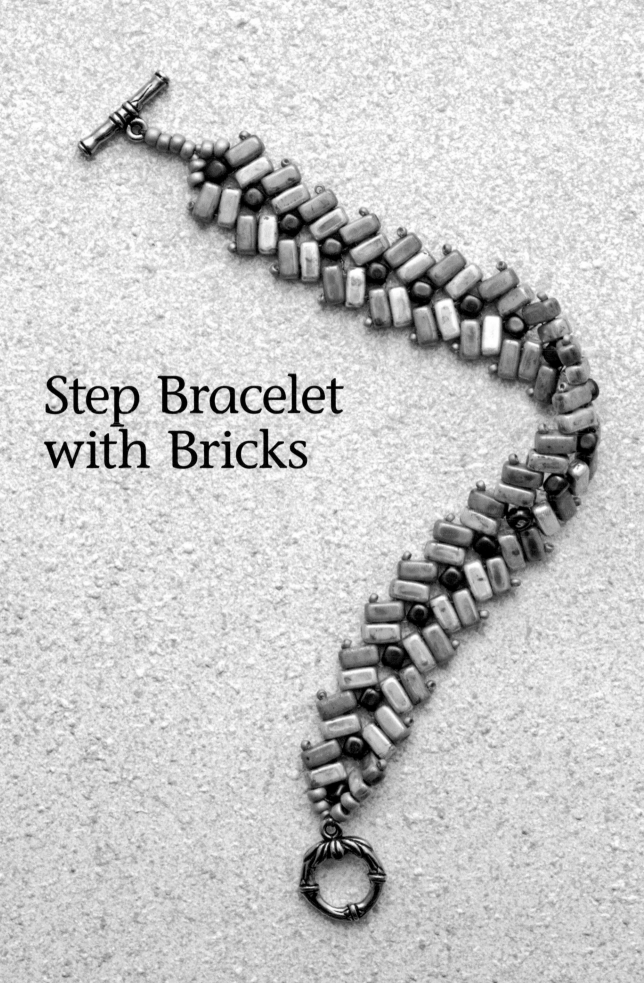

Step Bracelet
with Bricks

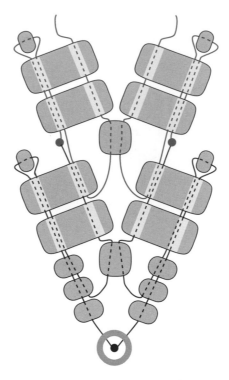

Figure

Step 1

Fold 2 yd. (1.8m) of thread in half and attach the center loop to one end of a clasp using a lark's head knot. Thread a needle on each end.

Step 2

[Figure, red thread] With either needle, pick up three 11º seed beads, two bricks, and a 15º seed bead. Turn and sew back through the same holes in the two bricks and two of the 11ºs. Pick up a cube, turn, and sew up through the open holes of the two bricks. Repeat on the other side with the other needle, but do not pick up a new cube; sew through the same cube.

Step 3

[Figure, blue thread] Pick up two bricks and a 15º. Turn, and sew back down through same holes of the two bricks; continue through the nearest hole of the previous brick. Pick up a cube, and sew through the open holes of the two new bricks just added. Repeat on the other side. Work as in step 2 until you reach the desired length. Attach the other half of the clasp. If you are using a toggle clasp, extend the bar with a few beads so you can get it through the loop.

MATERIALS

7 in. (18cm) bracelet

76 bricks

20 4mm Czech cubes

12 11º seed beads

40 15º seed beads

toggle clasp

2 yd. (1.8m) thread

: OPTIONS

Replace the bricks with half-Tilas or Rullas, or try a different bead in the center.

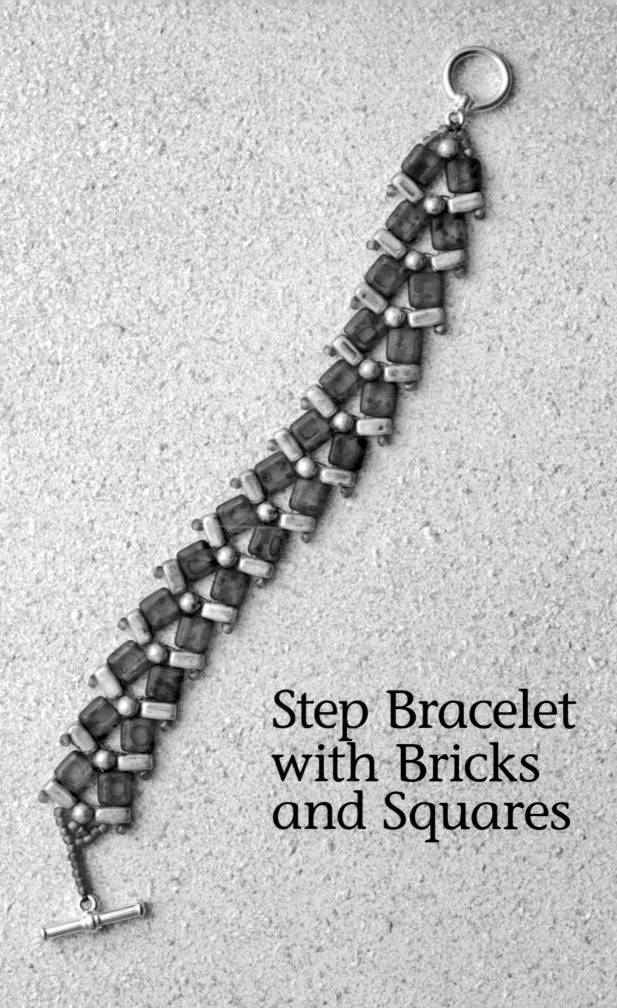

Step Bracelet
with Bricks
and Squares

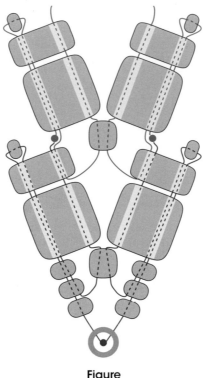

Figure

[Figure] Create a brick-and-square combination: The process is the same for this piece as in "Step Bracelet with Bricks," p. 48. Simply pick up a square and a brick instead of two bricks.

MATERIALS

7 in. (18cm) bracelet

26 bricks

26 squares

13 4mm round beads

35–45 15º seed beads

toggle clasp

2 yd. (1.8m) thread

: OPTIONS

Try a Tila and half-Tila in place of the square and brick.

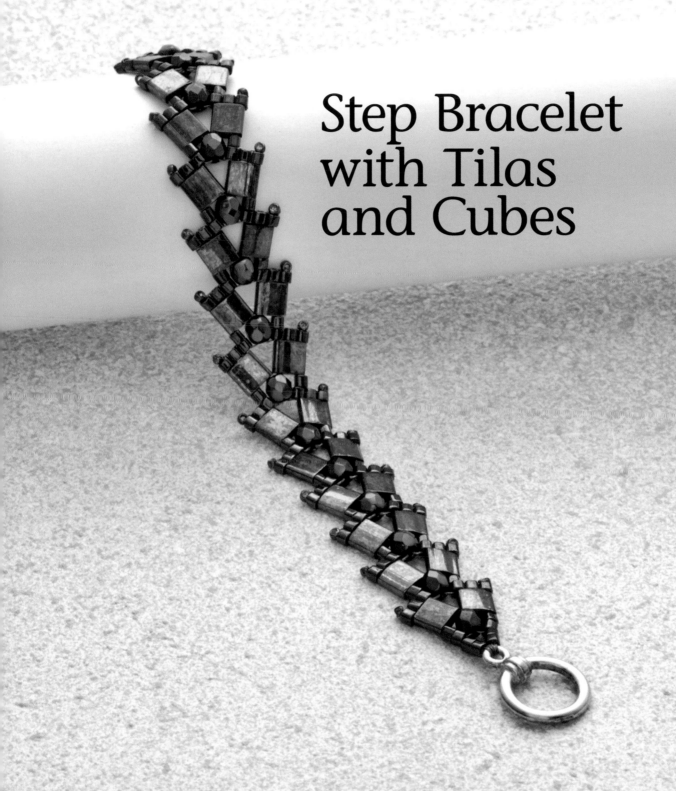

Step Bracelet
with Tilas
and Cubes

: OPTION
Replace the row of three cubes with a half-Tila.

Step 1

[Figure, red thread] Follow step 1 of "Step Bracelet with Bricks," p. 48. Then, pick up three cubes, and * pick up a 1.5mm cube, a Tila, and two cubes. Sew through the next-to-last cube again, and pull the thread to draw the two cubes side-by-side and down against the Tila. Pick up a 15º, turn, and sew back down through the outside hole of the Tila and two cubes. Pick up a 3mm fire-polished bead, turn, and sew up through the open hole of the Tila. Pick up a cube, and sew down through the adjacent cube and back up through the cube just added to make a three-cube row.

Step 2

[Figure, red thread] Repeat step 1 from the asterisk.

Step 3

[Figure, blue threads] Repeat the pattern on both sides alternately, or a few steps at a time, until you reach the desired length. Attach the bar of the toggle as in "Step Bracelet with Bricks."

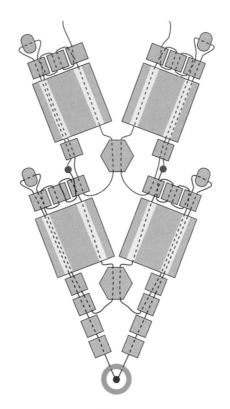

Figure

Note: Because this end is very pointed, you can simply attach the bar end of a toggle clasp.

MATERIALS

7 in. (18cm) bracelet

30 Tila beads

15 3mm fire-polished oval beads

2g 1.5mm cubes

30–40 15º seed beads

toggle clasp

2 yd. (1.8m) thread

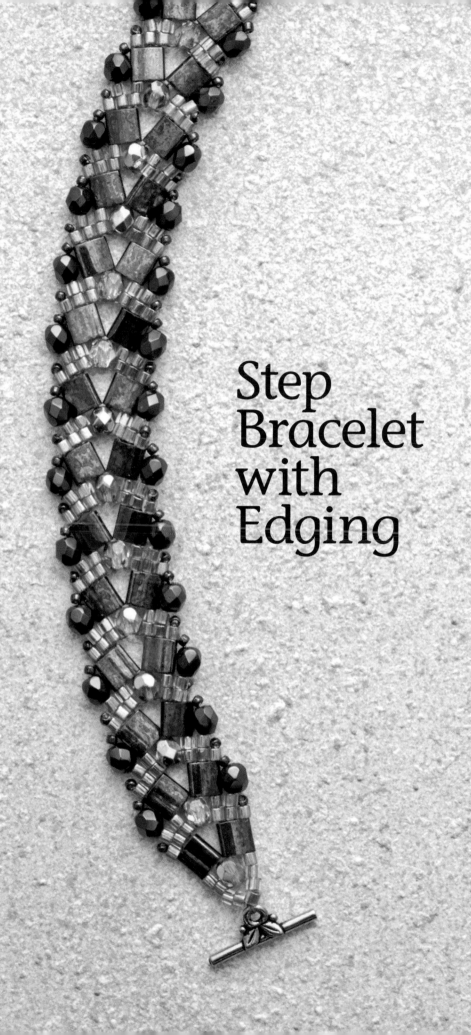

Step Bracelet with Edging

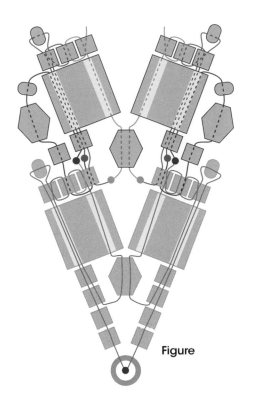

Figure

MATERIALS

6½ in. (16.5cm) bracelet

28 Tilas

42 4mm fire-polished
oval beads in **2** colors

2g 1.5mm cubes

28 15º seed beads

toggle clasp

2 yd. (1.8m) thread

: OPTIONS

For a different look,
use squares instead of
Tilas, rounds instead
of faceted ovals, and
Czech squares along
the edge.

With this bracelet, you'll start with the toggle bar end.

Step 1

[Figure, red thread] Follow step 1 of "Step Bracelet with Tilas and Cubes," p. 52, but after finishing the three-cube row, * pick up a cube, a Tila, a 15º seed bead, a 3mm fire-polished bead in the first color, and a cube. Sew down through the center cube in the three-cube row, turn, and sew up through the inside cube in the same row.

Step 2

[Figure, blue thread] Pick up a cube, a Tila, and two cubes. Sew through the next-to-last cube again, and pull the thread to draw the two cubes side-by-

side and down against the Tila. Pick up a 15º, turn, and sew back down through the cube, the outside hole of the Tila, and two cubes.

Step 3

[Figure, orange thread] Pick up a 3mm fire-polished bead in the second color, and sew up through the remaining hole of the Tila. Pick up a cube, and attach it to the second of the existing two cubes as before to make a three-cube row.

Step 4

Repeat the pattern on both sides, alternately or a few steps at a time, until you reach the desired length. Attach the loop end of the toggle.

Chapter 5
herringbone

It's easy to use the two holes of the two-hole beads in the same way you use the two beads in regular herringbone. Alternating squares with two bricks create a pretty basketweave pattern. A small bead at the intersection both adds a design element and hides the crossing threads that some beads leave visible. Begin your herringbone with a ladder base—or not, depending on your skill or style preference.

Herringbone designs with squares, Rullas, bricks, studs and even some round two-hole disks work very much the same. But herringbone with SuperDuos turns into a very tight, dense piece. I've used it for beaded beads and a bail, or broken up the density with large crystal beads for an elegant bracelet.

Herringbone Cuff with Squares and Rullas

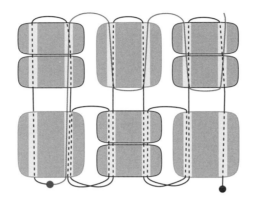

Figure 1

Step 1

[Figure 1, red thread] Thread a needle on a comfortable length of thread, and attach a stop bead, leaving a 10-in. (25cm) tail. Pick up a square and two Rullas. Turn, and sew back through the open holes of the two Rullas and the square. Pick up two Rullas, and sew down through the nearest hole of the square and back up through the same hole of the two new Rullas to attach them to the first square. Pick up a square, turn, and sew back down through the open hole of the same square, and the two open holes of the Rullas below. Pick up a square, and attach it to the two Rullas as before.

Pick up two Rullas, turn, and sew down through the open holes of the same two Rullas and the open hole of the square below.

Step 2

[Figure 1, blue thread] Turn and sew up through the right holes of the square and two Rullas in this column. Turn, and sew down through the nearest hole of the center square. Turn, and sew up through the other hole of the same square. Turn, and sew down through the nearest of the adjacent two Rullas, and sew up through the other hole of the same three Rullas.

MATERIALS

7 in. (18cm) bracelet

38 squares

74 Rullas

3-loop slide clasp

5 yd. (4.6m) thread

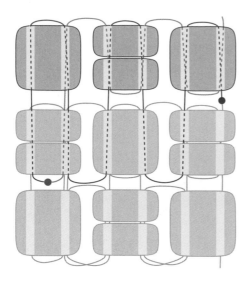

Figure 2

Step 3

[Figure 2, red thread] Begin the pattern: Pick up a square, turn, and sew down through the open hole of the same square. Continue down through the corresponding holes of the Rullas below. Turn, and sew up through the nearest hole of the center square. Pick up two Rullas, and sew down through the open holes of the same Rullas. Continue down through the corresponding hole of the center square. Turn, and sew up through the nearest holes of the adjacent Rullas. Pick up a square, turn, and sew down

through the open hole of the same square. Continue down through the corresponding holes of the Rullas below.

Step 4

[Figure 2, blue thread] Sew up through the other holes of the Rullas and the square in this column. Turn, and sew down through the nearest hole of the center Rullas. Turn, and sew up through the other holes of the same Rullas. Turn, and sew down through the nearest hole of the adjacent square, and then turn, and sew up through the other hole of the same square. This step closes the gap between the new beads and puts you in position to begin again. Work as in steps 3 and 4 until you reach the desired length.

Step 5

Sew half of a 3-loop slide clasp to each end of the bracelet (see photo), and end the threads.

: OPTIONS

Use any of these combinations to replace the squares: small studs, Tilas, two bricks, or two half-Tilas.

Herringbone Accented Cuff with Squares

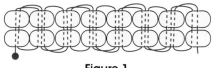

Figure 1

Step 1

[Figure 1] Thread a needle on a comfortable length of thread, and begin the ladder base: Pick up four 11º seed beads. Sew through the first two beads again in the same direction to form a box, leaving a 6-in. (15cm) tail. Sew through the second two 11ºs again in the same direction you went the first time. Pick up two more 11ºs. Sew through the previous beads (pair two) in the opposite direction and again through the new 11ºs in the same direction. Repeat until you have eight pairs.

MATERIALS

7 in. (18cm) bracelet

84 squares

56 11º seed beads

36 11º or 1.5mm cubes

52 15º seed beads

3-loop slide clasp

4 yd. (3.7m) thread (for ladder base)

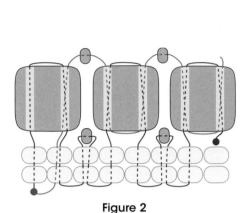

Figure 2

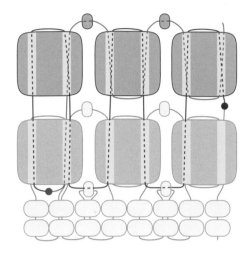

Figure 3

Step 2

[Figure 2, red thread] To simplify the illustration, I've made the thread used for the ladder invisible. Turn the ladder so the thread is exiting the last pair of beads on the right. Pick up a square, and pull it up against the work. Sew through the open hole of the square in the opposite direction, and continue through the pair of beads second from the right. Sew up through the third pair of beads from the right. Pick up a 15º seed bead, turn, and sew down through the same pair of beads. Turn and sew up through the fourth pair of beads. Pick up a square, sew down through the open hole, and continue through the fifth pair of beads. Turn, sew up through the sixth pair of beads, pick up a 15º, and sew down through the same pair. Sew up through the seventh pair of beads. Pick up a square, sew down through the open hole, and continue through the eighth pair of beads.

Step 3

[Figure 2, blue thread] Sew up through the seventh pair of beads and the corresponding hole of the end square. Pick up a 15º, and sew down through the nearest hole of the center square. Turn, and sew up through the other hole of the same square. Pick up a 15º, and sew down through the nearest hole of the next square. Turn, and sew up through the other hole of the same square. You are now in position to begin the pattern.

Step 4

[Figure 3, red thread] Establish the pattern: Pick up a square, and snug it up against the work. Sew through the open hole of the square in the opposite direction, and continue through the square below. Sew through the nearest 15º, and sew up through the nearest hole side of the center square in the row below the one you are working. Pick up another square, sew down through the open hole of the same square, and continue through the corresponding hole of the center square in the row

Note: Another way to start herringbone is on a ladder stitch base. I've built this one using 11º seed beads. Plus, I've added a small accent bead at the intersection of the threads.

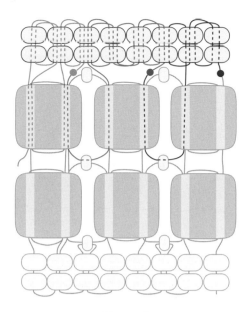

Figure 4

: OPTIONS

Two-hole disk beads work well in this design (if you can find them), and you can use a larger bead like an 8º seed bead as the accent bead. Another option is to start with a ladder base of 1.5mm cubes instead of the 11ºs.

below. Sew through the 15º, and then sew up through the nearest hole of the next square in the row below the one you are working. Pick up a square, sew down through the open hole of the same square, and continue through the corresponding hole of the left hole of the left square in the row below.

Step 5

[Figure 3, blue thread] Sew up through the right side of the left square in the row below, and the right side of the left square in the row you are working. Pick up a 15º, turn, and sew down through the left hole of the center square in the row you are working. Turn and sew up through the right hole of the same square. Pick up a 15º, turn, and sew down through the left hole of the right square, turn, and sew up through the right hole of the right square. Repeat steps 4 and 5 until you reach the desired length.

Step 6

[Figure 4, red thread] Create a closing ladder the same as the first one. Pick up four 11ºs, and sew through the first two 11ºs again to form a box. Sew down through the second pair again. Pick up two more 11ºs and attach them to the last pair. Sew down through the left hole of the right square on the last row, across through the 15º, and up through the right hole of the middle square of the last row.

Step 7

[Figure 4, blue thread] Sew up through the last two beads you attached. Attach two 11ºs three times, and continue down through the left hole of the middle square, across through the 15º, and up through the right hole of the left square.
[orange thread] Sew through the last pair you added. Attach two 11ºs two times, and continue down through the left hole of the left square. Sew half of a 3-loop bar clasp to each end (see photo), and end both threads.

Herringbone Bracelet with SuperDuos

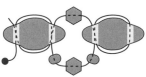

Figure 1

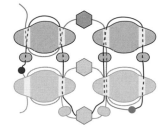

Figure 2

Step 1

[Figure 1] Thread a needle, and attach a stop bead on a comfortable length of thread, leaving an 8-in. (20cm) tail. Pick up a SuperDuo, and sew through the other hole in the opposite direction. Pick up a 15º seed bead, a 2mm crystal accent bead, a 15º, and a SuperDuo. Sew through the open hole of the SuperDuo in the opposite direction. Turn, and sew back through the first hole in the opposite direction. Pick up a 2mm, and sew down through the nearest hole of the first SuperDuo, and up through the other hole of the same SuperDuo in the opposite direction.

Step 2

[Figure 2, red thread] Pick up a 15º and a SuperDuo, and sew down through the open hole. Pick up a 15º, and continue down through the corresponding hole of the SuperDuo below. Skip the next 15º, and sew through the 2mm. Skip the next 15º, and sew up through the nearest hole

of the adjacent SuperDuo. Pick up a 15º and a SuperDuo, and sew down through the open hole of the same SuperDuo. Pick up a 15º, and continue through the corresponding hole of the SuperDuo below.

Step 3

[Figure 2, blue thread] Sew up through the other hole of the SuperDuo you just exited and continue through the 15º and the SuperDuo above. Pick up a 2mm, and sew down through the nearest hole of the adjacent SuperDuo. Continue through the other hole of the same SuperDuo in the opposite direction. Turn the work and repeat steps 2 and 3 twice for a total of six rows of SuperDuos.

Note: To ensure that your accent beads are spaced regularly, begin the work in the middle and work to either end. That way, you will always have a symmetrical bracelet.

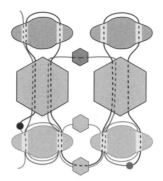

Figure 3

Step 4

[**Figure 3, red thread**] Add accent
beads: After you have completed
six rows (or however many you
desire), pick up a 6mm fire-polished
bead and a SuperDuo. Turn, sew down
through the open hole of the SuperDuo
in the opposite direction, and continue
through the accent bead. Sew down
through the corresponding hole of the
SuperDuo below, and continue through
the center 2mm and the nearest hole
of the adjacent SuperDuo. Pick up an
accent bead and a SuperDuo. Turn,
and sew down through the open hole
of the SuperDuo in the opposite direction and through the accent bead and
the open hole of the SuperDuo below.

Step 5

[**Figure 3, blue thread**] Sew up
through the other hole of the
SuperDuo you just exited, and
continue through the accent bead.
Pick up a 2mm, turn, and sew down
through the other accent bead, and
continue through the nearest hole of
the SuperDuo below. Turn, and sew up
through the other hole of the same
SuperDuo, the fire-polished bead, and
the corresponding hole of the new
SuperDuo. Repeat steps 2–5 until you
reach the desired length.

Step 6

Sew a clasp half to the center beads
on each end of the bracelet, and end
the threads.

MATERIALS

7 in. (18cm) bracelet

12 6mm fire-polished
   oval beads

49 2mm crystal accent
   beads

84 SuperDuos

1g 15º seed beads

magnetic clasp

2 yd. (1.8m) thread

: OPTION
Use any kind of bead that will fit for your accent.

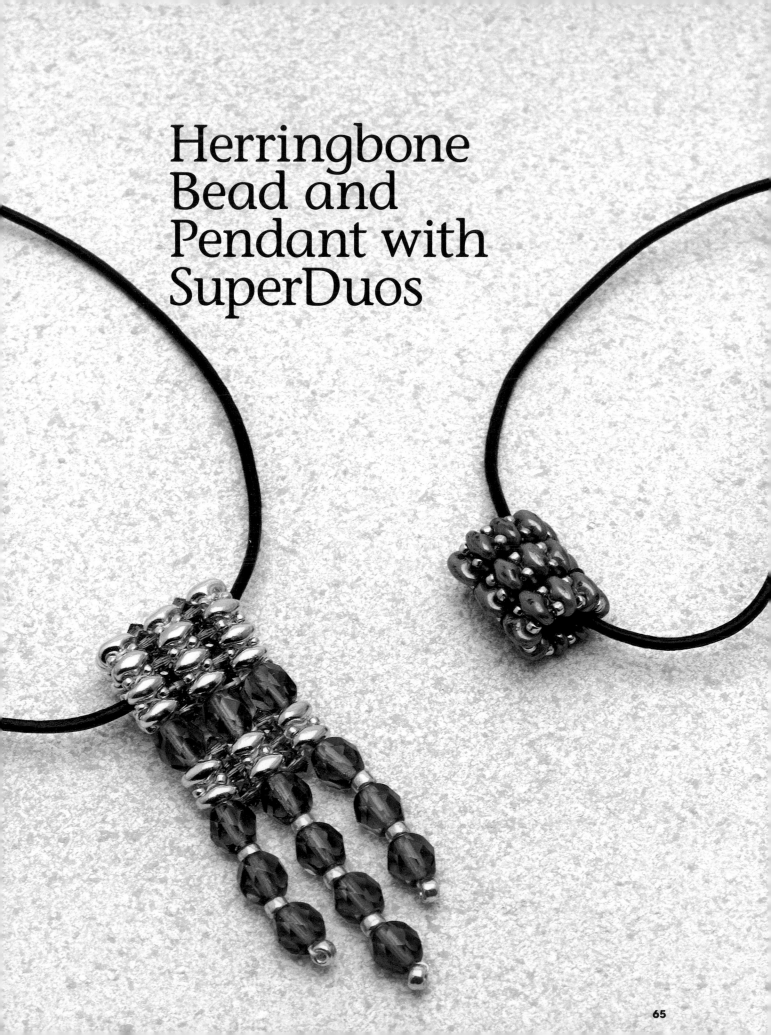

Herringbone Bead and Pendant with SuperDuos

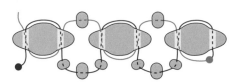

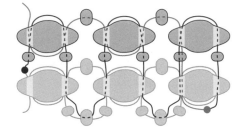

Figure 1   Figure 2

Note: This is such a tight little stitch that you will want to switch to a finer thread, like 8-lb. or 5-lb. test, and a size 11 or 12 beading needle.

Step 1

[Figure 1, red thread] Thread a needle on a comfortable length of thread, pick up a SuperDuo, and sew through the other hole in the opposite direction. Pick up a 15º seed bead, an 11º seed bead, a 15º, and a SuperDuo, and sew through the other hole of this SuperDuo in the opposite direction. Pick up a 15º, an 11º, a 15º, and a SuperDuo, and sew through the other hole of this SuperDuo.

Step 2

[Figure 1, blue thread] Sew back up through the other hole of the SuperDuo your thread is exiting. Pick

up an 11º, sew through the nearest hole of the middle SuperDuo, and continue through the other hole of the same SuperDuo. Pick up an 11º, sew through the nearest hole of the next SuperDuo, and continue through the other hole of the same SuperDuo.

Step 3

[Figure 2, red thread] Begin the pattern: Pick up a 15º and a SuperDuo, and sew through the open hole of the SuperDuo in the opposite direction. Snug the beads up to the work. Pick up a 15º, and sew down through the corresponding hole of the SuperDuo in the previous row, skip the next 15º, and sew through the 11º, skip the next 15º, and sew up through the nearest hole of the middle SuperDuo. Pick up a 15º and a SuperDuo, and sew through

MATERIALS

½x⁵⁄₁₆ in. (13x8mm) bead

24 SuperDuos

48 15º seed beads

40 11º seed beads

1 yd. (.9m) thread

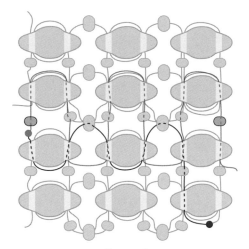

Figure 3

the other hole of the SuperDuo in the opposite direction. Snug the beads up to the work. Pick up a 15º, and sew down through the hole below in the previous row. Sew through the 11º, turn, and sew up.

Step 4

[Figure 2, blue thread] Sew up through the other hole of the SuperDuo you just exited and through the 15º and the SuperDuo above. Pick up an 11º. Turn and sew down and then back up through the middle SuperDuo. Pick up an 11º, turn, and sew down and up through the last SuperDuo. Repeat steps 3 and 4 until you reach the desired length (I stitched eight rows for my bead)

Step 5

[Figure 3, red thread] Join the ends. Make the second pass (step 4) in which you pick up the 11º beads from the other end.

Step 6

[Figure 3, blue thread] Make another first pass (step 3), incorporating the SuperDuos from the other end and picking up the missing 15ºs at either side (orange beads).

: OPTIONS

Make your bead long enough to reach around a napkin for an elegant napkin ring. Make a bail by joining the piece as if for a bead, but continue with the herringbone and add a fringe.

Chapter 6

crossweave

Crossweaving is a fast, intuitive technique that I like to use while creating necklaces. I've focused on the "business end" of the necklace, the front part that shows the most. (And it's much faster and easier than an entire collar!) My favorite is the triple dagger, but because two-hole daggers are less accessible, I've also included a version that uses one-hole daggers.

I often wish I didn't have to add thread, so I've given you a way to work an entire necklace with a single long thread. A simple crossweave technique starts with a strand of beads centered on a long thread. Then you work back and forth with the threads and finally use the ends to create the necklace side straps.

SuperDuo and Two-Hole Dagger Necklace

MATERIALS

18½ in. (47cm) necklace

42 16mm two-hole daggers

57 SuperDuos in **2** colors

4g 8º seed beads in **2** colors

2g 11º seed beads in **2** colors

toggle clasp

4 yd. (3.7m) thread

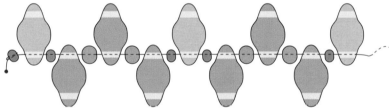

Figure 1

Step 1

[Figure 1] Cut 3½–4 yd. (3.2–3.7m) of thread. Attach a stop bead in the center, and thread a needle on one end. Pick up a SuperDuo and an 11º seed bead. Pick up a repeating pattern of: a SuperDuo, an 8º seed bead, a SuperDuo, an 8º, a SuperDuo, an 11º, a SuperDuo, and an 11º until you reach the desired length. (My centerpiece is 15 segments long.) End with an 11º and a SuperDuo. Center the whole length on the thread, moving the stop bead to accommodate the new placement.

PUT A STOP TO IT

The SuperDuos will turn any which way, and they won't all settle into place until you have finished stringing. If you have trouble corralling the loose SuperDuos, run a temporary thread through the empty holes of every other SuperDuo, starting with the first and ending with the last. Attach stop beads to each end to hold the beads in place until you are ready for the final stringing.

Step 2

[Figure 2, red thread] Pick up an 11º and an 8º. Sew back through the open hole of the second SuperDuo. * Pick up an 8º, a two-hole dagger, an 8º, a dagger, and an 8º. Skip the Super-Duo, and sew through the open hole of the next SuperDuo. Pick up an 11º and an 8º. Sew through the same hole of the next SuperDuo you sewed through in the previous step. Sew back through the 8º you just picked up, pull the thread taut, and position the 8º so it sits at the base of the SuperDuo. Pick up an 11º, and sew through the empty hole of the next SuperDuo. Repeat from the asterisk across the strung beads, sewing through every-other SuperDuo. After you sew through the next-to-last SuperDuo, pick up an 8º and an 11º.

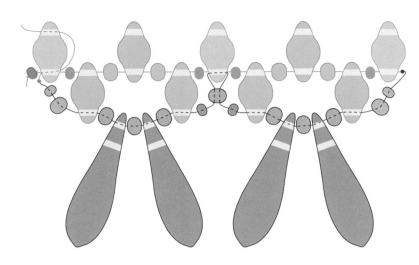

Figure 2

Step 3

[Figure 2, blue thread] Turn and sew back through the bottom hole of the very first SuperDuo you picked up, and continue through the top hole of the same SuperDuo in the opposite direction. Attach a stop bead on this thread while you work with the tail.

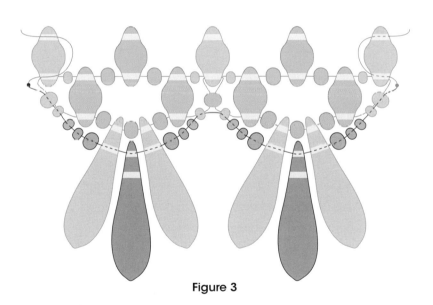

Figure 3

Step 4

[Figure 3, red thread] Remove the first stop bead, and sew down through the 8º and 11º added in step 2. * Pick up two 11ºs and an 8º. Sew through the lower hole of the first dagger, pick up a new dagger, and sew through the lower hole of the next dagger. Pick up an 8º and two 11ºs. Sew through the two 11º under the 8º. Repeat from the asterisk until you have sewn through all the sets of daggers.

Step 5

[Figure 3, blue thread] After you pick up the last 8º and two 11ºs, sew through the 11º and 8º at the end of the last row. Turn and sew back through the lower hole of the last SuperDuo. Turn again and sew through the upper hole.

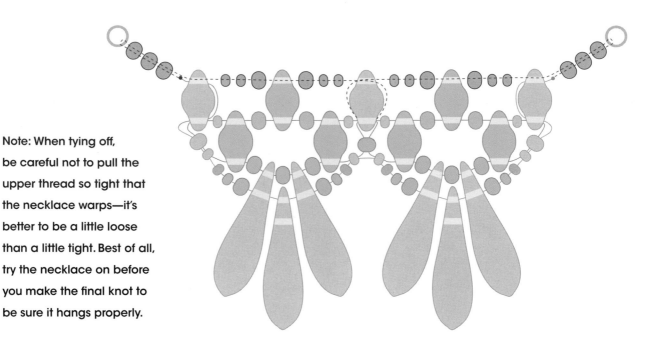

Note: When tying off, be careful not to pull the upper thread so tight that the necklace warps—it's better to be a little loose than a little tight. Best of all, try the necklace on before you make the final knot to be sure it hangs properly.

Figure 4

Step 6

[Figure 4] With either thread, string as many beads as you need to reach the rest of the way around your neck, depending on how long you want the necklace to be. Sew through one half of a clasp, and sew back through all of the beads to the nearest SuperDuo.

Step 7

(If you have tied on a temporary thread, remove it now.) Continue stringing through the open holes of the remaining SuperDuos using this pattern: Pick up two 11°s and an 8°, and sew through the open hole of the next SuperDuo. Pick up an 8° and two 11°s, and sew through the open hole of the next SuperDuo. Continue in this pattern until you are halfway across.

Step 8

With the other thread, work as in steps 6 and 7 to make a mirror image on the other half of the necklace. Continue both threads back through the work to meet in the middle. End them there.

Square, SuperDuo, and One-Hole Dagger Collar

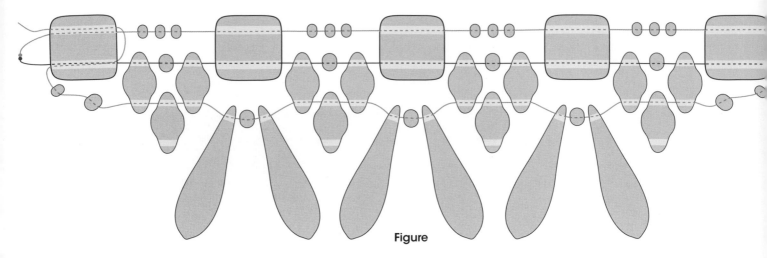

Figure

Step 1

[Figure, red thread] Center a stop bead on 4 yd. (3.7m) of thread. Thread a needle on one end, and pick up a repeating pattern of a square, a SuperDuo, an 8º seed bead, and a SuperDuo until you have 14 squares, ending with the square. Center the group of beads on the thread, moving the stop bead as necessary.

Step 2

[Figure, blue thread] Pick up an 11º seed bead and an 8º. * Sew through the open hole of the last SuperDuo, pick up a SuperDuo, and sew through the open hole of the next SuperDuo. Pick up a dagger, an 8º, and a dagger. Repeat from the asterisk until you have sewn through all the beads. Pick up an 8º and an 11º, and sew through the same hole of the first square, with the needle pointing toward the other end of the beadwork. Turn, and sew through the open hole of the same square, with the needle pointing toward the tail. Attach a stop bead.

Step 3

[Figure, orange thread] Remove the first stop bead, and sew through the upper hole of the first square. Pick up three 11ºs, and sew through the open hole of the next square. Repeat until you have sewn through the open hole of the squares.

Step 4

Finish the necklace: Your threads are now exiting the top hole of the squares on each end. Check that your thread is not loose anywhere; tighten it up and remove any stop beads as needed. String beads equally on each thread to complete the entire length of your necklace. Pick up a clasp half on each end, and sew back through the straps into the body of the necklace. End the threads.

MATERIALS

15½ in. (39.4cm) collar

14 Tila beads

39 SuperDuos

24 one-hole daggers

1g 8º seed beads

1g 11º seed beads

beads for stringing

magnetic clasp

4 yd. (3.7m) thread

Note: I like to cross the threads in the center and make a second pass out to the clasp ends and back, just so the necklace is not hanging by a single thread. Because you started with 4 yd. (3.7m) of thread, you should have plenty left to do this.

Brick
Criss-Cross
Collar

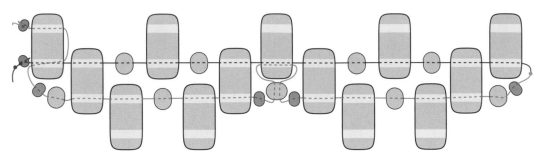

Figure 1

Step 1

[Figure 1, red thread] Attach a stop bead to the center of 4 yd. (3.7m) of thread, and thread a needle on one end. Pick up two bricks. Pick up a repeating pattern of an 8º seed bead, a brick, an 8º, and three bricks until you reach the desired length, ending with the first two bricks of a group of three. Center the beads on the thread, moving the stop bead to accommodate the new placement. Each end brick and every other brick in between will turn up. Snug the beads.

Step 2

[Figure 1, blue thread] Work the second row below the first with the needle pointing toward the tail. Pick up an 11º seed bead and an 8º, skip the first brick, and sew through the open hole of the next brick. * Pick up a brick, an 8º, and a brick. Skip the 8º, brick, and 8º in the previous row, and sew through the open hole of the next brick. Pick up an 11º and an 8º, and sew through the bottom hole (the hole with the thread already in it) of the next brick. Sew back through the 8º. Pull the 8º up and center it against the bottom of the brick. Pick up an 11º and sew through the open hole of the next brick. Repeat from the asterisk until you sew through the next-to-last bead. Pick up an 8º and an 11º. Sew back through the bottom hole (the one with the thread already in it) of the last bead with the needle pointing toward the other end of the beadwork. Sew through the open hole of the same brick. Attach a stop bead while you work with the other thread.

MATERIALS

15 in. (38cm) collar

162 bricks

6g 8º seed beads

3g 11º seed beads

2 3mm soldered jump rings

2 3mm open jump rings

magnetic clasp

4 yd. (3.7m) thread

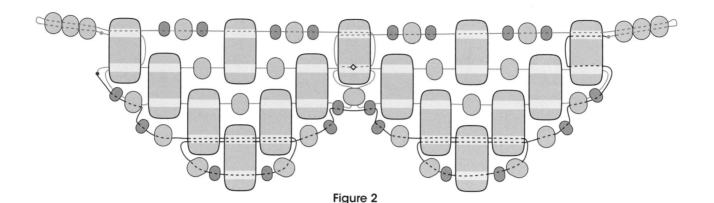

Figure 2

Step 3

[Figure 2, red thread] Remove the first stop bead and thread a needle on the tail. Sew back through the 11º and 8º you added in the previous step. * Pick up an 11º and an 8º. Sew through the open hole of the next brick (the third over). Pick up a brick, skip the 8º in the second row, and sew through the open hole of the next brick. Turn, pick up an 8º and an 11º, and sew through the open hole of the newest brick added in this step. Pick up an 11º and an 8º. Turn, and sew through the same holes of the three bricks just added in the same direction. Pick up an 8º and an 11º. Sew through the two 11ºs on either side of the 8º attached to the first row. Repeat from the asterisk. Sew up through the 8º and 11º at the other end. Sew in and out of the last brick in the first row.

Step 4

[Figure 2, blue thread] Each thread will now be exiting the top hole of the last brick on each end. On each end, pick up a soldered jump ring and sew back through the other hole of the brick. Retrace the thread path. With each thread, sew back through the top of the end brick, pick up a group of an 11º, an 8º, and an 11º, and continue through the open hole of the next brick in the first row. Repeat across the necklace with each thread, meeting in the middle. Ease the tension so the necklace bends easily around the neck but doesn't warp or pucker, and end the threads.

: OPTION

Try this same design with two-hole bars. You will need to add a few more seed beads to reach across the bar at the ends. You can also add drops instead of the final two-hole bead at the point.

Chapter 7
right-angle weave

Why is right-angle weave considered so difficult? I think it's because you are constantly turning. This can lead to losing your place, losing your patience, and, maybe worst of all, losing your tension. You can turn your hand or the work, but most often it's a combination of the two.

However you work this out, you really have to start thinking in circles. And when you build a circle of beads, you can come off the circle in as many directions as you have major beads. This lets you go in a straight line, create parallel rows, or angle off in a number of directions.

As a stitch, right-angle weave is a kind of chameleon. It can look very different, depending on how it twists and turns. These interesting designs are a good reason to master this stitch!

Right-Angle Weave Bracelet with SuperDuos

Figure 1

MATERIALS

7 in. (18cm) bracelet

152 SuperDuos

2g 11º seed beads

toggle clasp

4 yd. (3.7m) thread

Note: This weaving will be very loose and flexible until you add the edging.

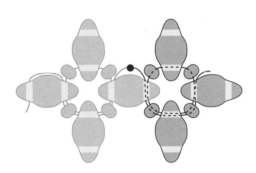

Figure 2

Step 1

[Figure 1] On a comfortable length of thread, thread a needle and pick up a SuperDuo. Continue through the open hole of the SuperDuo in the opposite direction, leaving a 6-in. (15cm) tail. * Pick up an 11º seed bead, a SuperDuo, an 11º, a SuperDuo, an 11º, a Super-Duo, and an 11º. Sew through the first SuperDuo again to form a ring. Continue through the next 11º, SuperDuo, 11º, and SuperDuo to exit the SuperDuo opposite the tail. This creates one right-angle weave unit.

Step 2

[Figure 2] Sew through the open hole of the same SuperDuo in the opposite direction. Repeat step 1 from the asterisk to form a second right-angle weave unit. Continue in right-angle weave until you have a strip the desired length.

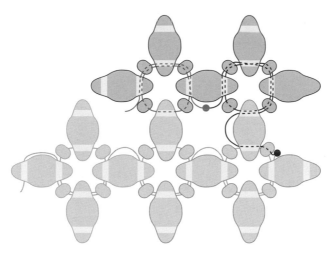

Figure 3

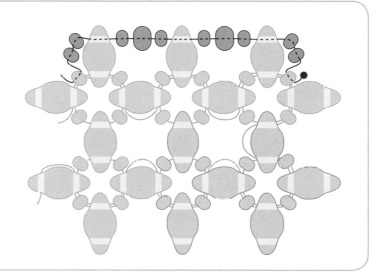

Note: You could just fill the space between the SuperDuos with beads, but this is a loose weave and benefits from the stiffness of this denser edging, shown in the figure. Be sure not to pull the edging so tight that it warps the bracelet.

Step 3

[Figure 3, red thread] Add a row: Continue around the ring of beads until you reach the SuperDuo you want to start a new row from. Turn and sew through the open hole of this SuperDuo. Pick up an 11º, a SuperDuo, an 11º, a SuperDuo, an 11º, a SuperDuo, and an 11º. Sew through the SuperDuo your thread exited in the previous row, and continue through the next six beads in the new unit.

Step 4

[Figure 3, blue thread] Pick up an 11º, a SuperDuo, an 11º, a SuperDuo, and an 11º, and sew through the open hole of the adjacent SuperDuo added in the previous row. Retrace the thread path through the next six beads. Sew through the open hole of this SuperDuo. Repeat this step until you reach the desired length.

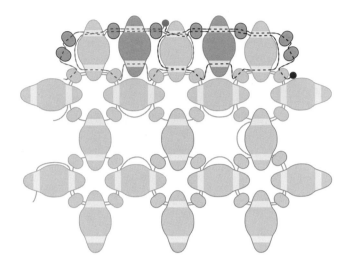

Figure 4

Step 5

[Figure 4, red thread] To finish the long edges: Exit the outside corner 11º. Pick up two 11ºs, and sew through the open hole of the first SuperDuo along a long edge of the bracelet. * Pick up an 11º, a SuperDuo, and an 11º, and sew through the open hole of the next SuperDuo. Turn, and sew through the other hole of the same SuperDuo, with the needle pointing in the opposite direction. Sew through the 11º at the base SuperDuo, the open hole of the SuperDuo you just picked up, and the 11º, and continue through the adjacent hole of the end SuperDuo. Retrace the thread path through the first seven beads in this step to exit the third SuperDuo along this edge.

Step 6

[Figure 4, blue thread] Work as in step 5 to add an 11º, a SuperDuo, and an 11º between each right-angle weave unit along the edge of the bracelet. When you reach the end, pick up two 11ºs and sew in through the outside corner 11º of the other end. Cross to the other side and repeat.

Step 7

Attach a clasp half to each end of the bracelet (see photo). End the threads.

: OPTIONS

I don't recommend making this piece with bricks, Rullas, or squares. It is so floppy, you can hardly manage it. In this case, stick to the SuperDuos.

Right-Angle Weave Bracelet and Necklace with Bricks

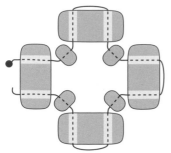

Figure 1

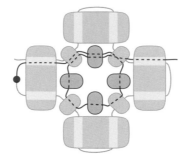

Figure 2

Note: If you study this stitch, you can see that this is a kind of reverse right-angle weave. Instead of arranging the beads to face out of the circle, these beads face *into* the circle.

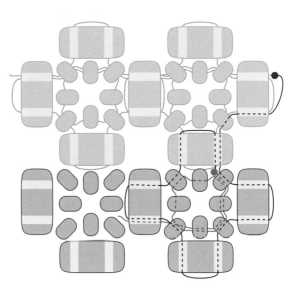

Figure 3

Step 1

[**Figure 1**] On a comfortable length of thread, pick up a brick. * Pick up an 11º seed bead and a brick, and sew through the open hole of the brick. Repeat from the asterisk twice, and then pick up an 11º, and sew through the open hole of the first brick.

Step 2

[**Figure 2**] Turn and sew through the first hole of the brick your thread is exiting and continue on through the first 11º. Pick up an 11º and sew through the next 11º. Repeat this stitch three times to add an 11º between each corner 11º. Continue through the first 11º added in this step, the next corner 11º, and the nearest hole of the brick.

Step 3

Repeat step 1 from the asterisk and step 2 until you reach the desired length.

Finishing the Bracelet

Step 4

[**Figure 3, red thread**] Add a row: Sew into the other hole of the brick your thread is exiting, and continue through the adjacent corner 11º and the nearest hole of the adjacent brick. Pick up an 11º and a brick, turn, and sew into the open hole of the same brick. Repeat this stitch twice. Pick up an 11º, and sew up into the nearest hole of the adjacent brick, turn, and sew down through the other hole of the same brick.

MATERIALS

7 in. (18cm) bracelet

97 bricks

2g 8º seed beads

4g 11º seed beads

toggle clasp

3 yd. (2.7m) thread

16 in. (41cm) necklace

97 bricks

3g 6º seed beads

3g 8º seed beads

4g 11º seed beads

4½ in. (11.4cm) chain

hook clasp

3 yd. thread

Figure 4

Step 5

[Figure 3, blue thread] Sew through the adjacent corner 11º. Pick up an 11º, and sew through the next corner 11º. Repeat this stitch to complete the round, and sew through the upper left corner 11º and continue on through the next five 11ºs to the lower left corner 11º. Sew through the nearest hole of the brick. Continue to repeat the pattern, incorporating all the lower bricks in the previous row. Repeat until you finish matching the first row.

Step 6

[Figure 4] Exit the outside hole of the last brick along the edge. Pick up two 11ºs, and sew through the other hole of the same brick. Turn, and sew back through the first hole of the same brick and the two 11ºs just added. Pick up an 11º and an 8º seed bead. * Sew through the top hole of the vertical brick below with the needle pointed toward the nearest end. Sew back through the 8º you just picked up, with the needle pointed in the opposite direction. Pick up three 11ºs, and attach the last two to the brick below as shown in the figure. Pick up an 11º and an 8º. Repeat from the asterisk. Finish by attaching the two 11ºs as before. Repeat this step along the other edge.

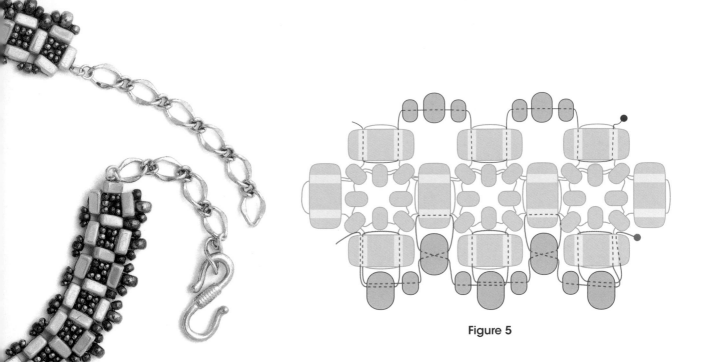

Figure 5

Step 7

Attach a clasp half to each end of the bracelet (see photo). End the threads.

Note: To make the beadwork curve into a necklace, you will need to tighten one side and spread the other. Do the tightening stitch along the side that has the double thread in the three 11°s. You'll notice that the piece tends to bend in more easily on this side. Step 6 tightens the upper side, while step 2 spreads the lower side.

Finishing the Necklace

Alternate step 4

[Figure 5, red thread] Exit the inside hole of the corner horizontal brick. * Pick up an 11°, an 8°, and an 11°. Sew down and back up through the holes of the next horizontal brick. Repeat from the asterisk until you finish the upper side.

Alternate step 5

[Figure 5, blue thread] Exit the outside hole of the last brick along the lower edge. Pick up a 6° seed bead, sew through the other hole of the same brick, turn, and sew back through the first hole of the same brick and continue through the 6°. Pick up an 8° and a 6°. * Sew through the bottom hole of the vertical brick above, with the needle pointing toward the nearest end. Sew back through the 6° you just picked up, with the needle pointing in the opposite direction. Pick up an 8° and a 6°, and attach the 6° to the brick below as shown in the figure. Pick up an 8° and a 6°. Repeat from the asterisk.

Alternate step 6

Attach a 2-in. (5cm) piece of chain to each end of the necklace, and attach a hook clasp to one end. End the threads.

Right-Angle Weave Bracelet with Large Studs and Squares

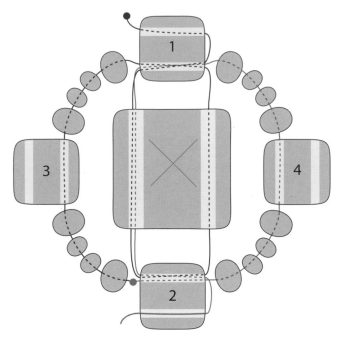

Figure 1

MATERIALS

7¼ in. (18.4cm) bracelet

10 12mm studs

47 squares

2g 8º seed beads

2g 11º seed beads

2-loop slide clasp

3 yd. (2.7m) thread

Note: If you prefer to use two needles, see the sidebar for an alternate step 1 and 2.

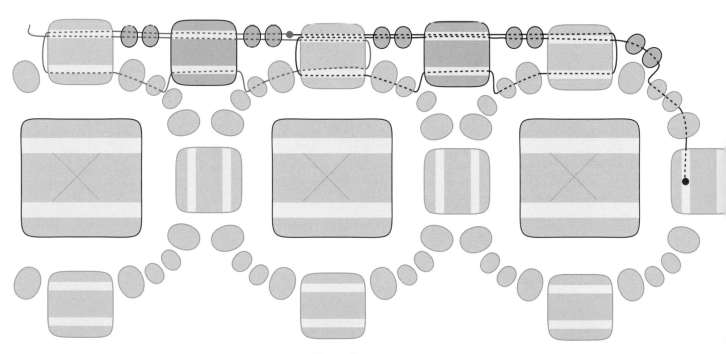

Figure 2

Step 1

[Figure 1, red thread] To work this piece with one needle, attach a stop bead on a comfortable length of thread, leaving an 8-in. (20cm) tail. Pick up a square, turn, and sew through the open hole of the square in the opposite direction. * Pick up a large stud, making sure the top is facing up, and a square. Turn, and sew through the open hole of the stud. Sew through the lower hole of the first square in the same direction as the first pass. Pick up an 8º seed bead, two 11º seed beads, an 8º, a square, an 8º, two 11ºs, and an 8º.

Using Two Needles

Alternate step 1

[Figure, red thread] Fold 3 yd. (2.7m) of thread in half and attach the folded end to a clasp with a lark's head knot. Thread a needle on each end, and add enough spacer beads to meet the two holes of the first square. With either needle, pick up a square, turn, and sew through the open hole of the square in the opposite direction. Pick up a large stud, making sure the top is facing up, pick up a square, turn and sew through the other hole of the stud in the opposite direction. Sew through the lower hole of the first square in the same direction. Pick up an 8º, two 11ºs, an 8º, a square, an 8º, two 11ºs, and an 8º. Continue through the upper hole of the bottom square, turn, and sew in the opposite direction through the bottom hole of the same square. Attach a temporary stop bead here, if needed

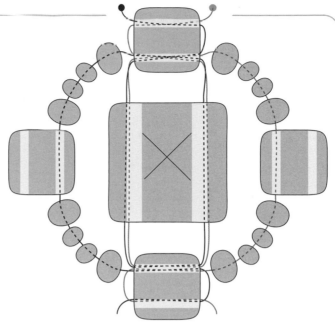

Alternate step 2

[Figure, blue thread] Sew through the first square from the other side and mirror the thread action in step 1. Repeat until you have the desired length.

Step 2

[Figure 1, blue thread] Sew through the upper hole of the second square. Pick up an 8º, two 11ºs, an 8º, a square, an 8º, two 11ºs, and an 8º. Continue through the bottom hole of the first square and the left hole of the stud. Sew through the upper hole of the second square, turn, and sew through the open hole of the same square. You are now in position to repeat from the asterisk in step 1. Continue until you reach the desired length.

Step 3

[Figure 2, red thread] Exit the inner hole of the end square, and sew through the 8º and two 11ºs. Pick up two 11ºs, and sew through the outer hole of the first square along the edge. * Pick up two 11ºs, a square, and two 11ºs, and sew through the outer hole of the next square along the edge. Turn and sew back through the inner hole of the same square, and continue through the 8º and 11º. Sew through the open hole of the new square, the 11º, the 8º, and the inner hole of the first square. Turn, and sew back through the other hole of the same square, the two 11ºs, the new square, two 11ºs, and the following square.

Step 4

[Figure 2, blue thread] Repeat from the asterisk in step 3 until you have created an edge along both sides. Be careful not to pull the edge too tight and create a warp on either side of the bracelet. Repeat on the other side, end the thread, and attach the other end of the clasp.

Chapter 8
cluster stitch

The cluster stitch is my new variation on right-angle weave. However, instead of just gathering beads into a round, you loop your way around the round, picking up and interlocking center beads. Then to make it more complex, you add a second cluster that alternates with the first, which has a inner circulation of its own. This stitch can seem a little complicated, so I've started this section with a very simple version for beginners.

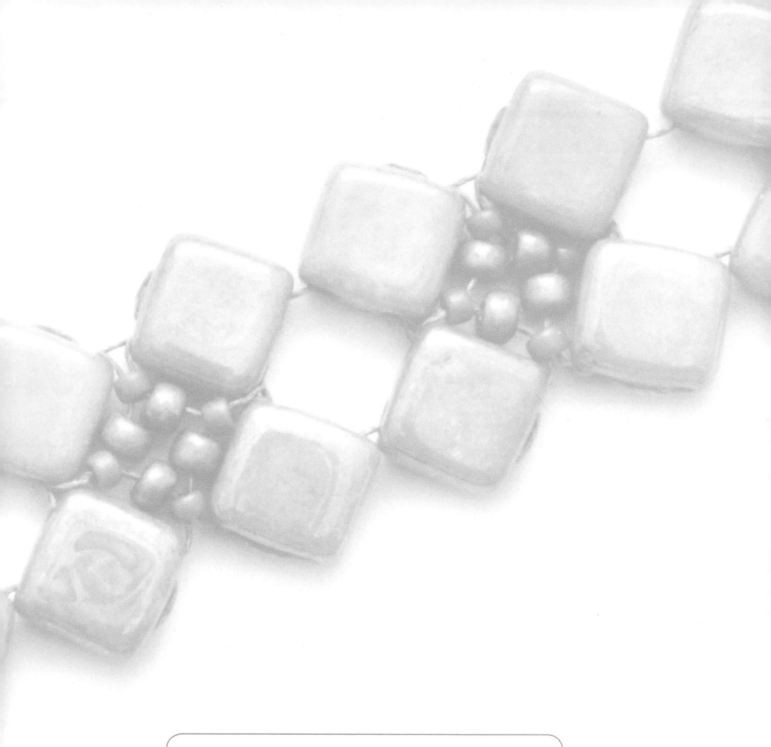

This brand-new stitch is exciting to work and rewards you with many opportunities for expression and expansion. I've had so much fun exploring this stitch, I've included a gallery of further options so you can see what beautiful possibilities lie in store for you when you master cluster stitch!

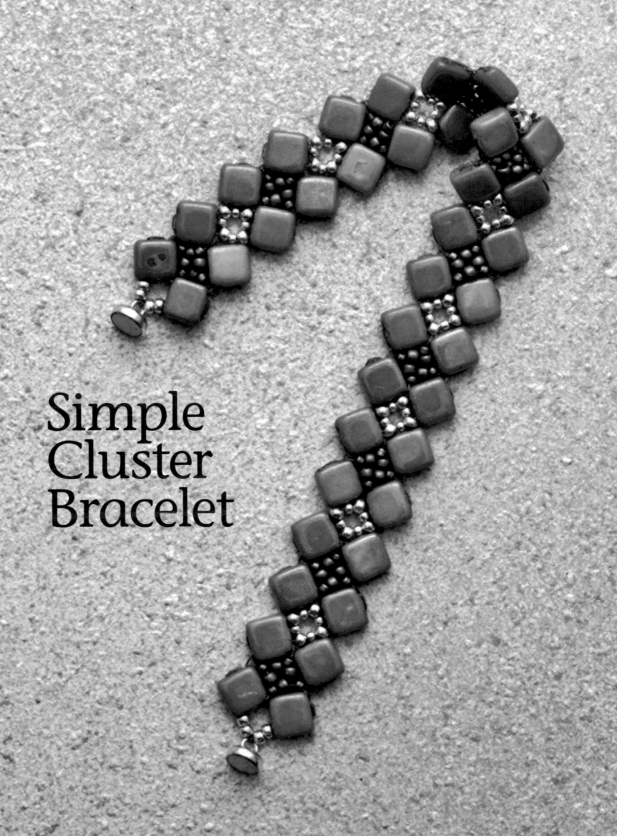

Simple
Cluster
Bracelet

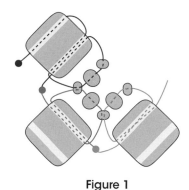

Figure 1

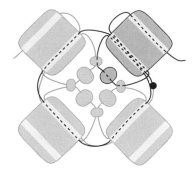

Figure 2

Note: Choose this version if you're a new beader, but if you have some experience and feel confident, go ahead and start with the regular version so you won't have to "unlearn" this one.

Step 1
[Figure 1, red thread] Thread a needle on a comfortable length of thread, pick up a square, turn, and sew through the open hole of the same square, leaving a 6-in. (15cm) tail. Pick up a 15º seed bead, an 11º seed bead, and a 15º. Sew back through the same hole of the square again in the same direction.

Step 2
[Figure 1, blue thread] Pick up a square, a 15º, and an 11º. Sew through the first 15º you picked up in the previous step. Sew through the same hole of the square you just exited.

Step 3
[Figure 1, orange thread] Repeat step 2.

Step 4
[Figure 2] Pick up a square. Sew through the nearest 15º added in step 1. Pick up an 11º, and sew through the nearest 15º added in step 3. Sew back through the hole of the square you just exited, and continue through the inner holes of all four squares to exit the square added in this step. Turn and sew through the open hole of this square.

MATERIALS
7 in. (18cm) bracelet
40 squares
1g 11º seed beads in
   2 colors
1g 15º seed beads in
   2 colors
magnet clasp
3 yd. (2.7m) thread

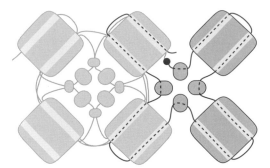

Figure 3

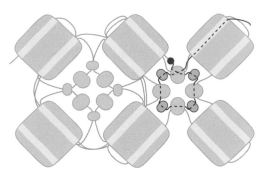

Figure 4

Step 5

[**Figure 3**] Use seed beads in a different color for steps 5 and 6. Pick up an 11º and a square, and sew through the open hole of the same square in the opposite direction. Snug the beads up to the work. Repeat the stitch once. Pick up an 11º, and sew through the open hole of the adjacent square in the previous cluster. Turn, and sew through the other hole in the same square. Pick up an 11º, sew through the inner hole of the next square in the previous cluster, turn, and sew through the other hole in the same square.

Step 6

[**Figure 4**] Sew through the first 11º added in the previous step, pick up a 15º, and sew through the next 11º in the ring. Repeat this stitch three times, and continue through the nearest hole of the first square added in step 5. You are in position to begin again from step 1. Repeat steps 1–6 until you reach the desired length.

Step 7

To attach the clasp, exit an end square, pick up two 11ºs, half of the clasp, and two 11ºs, and sew into the adjacent end square. Repeat on the other end.

: OPTIONS

If you want an even simpler version, make the same pass as in step 5 but don't pick up the 11º seed beads, continue into the new upper square, and start again with step 1. Try this bracelet with Tilas.

Advanced Cluster Bracelet with Squares

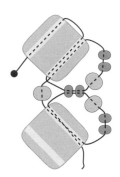

Figure 1

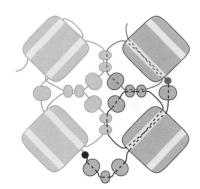

Figure 2

Note: If you're an intermediate beader, go ahead and start with this stitch rather than the basic. This version adds some beads around the outside of the cluster, which opens up the cluster and makes room for larger beads in the center. You'll use 11º and 8º seed beads instead of 15º and 11º seed beads in the center of the clusters.

Step 1

[Figure 1] Thread a needle on 2 yd. (3.7m) of thread. Pick up a square, and sew through the open hole of the same square, leaving a 6-in. (15cm) tail. Pick up two 11º seed beads, an 8º seed bead, and two 11ºs. Sew back through the same hole of the square in the same direction. Pick up an 8º, a square, two 11ºs, and an 8º, and sew through the first two 11ºs in the previous stitch on the same hole of the square you just added. Pull all the beads together snugly.

Step 2

[Figure 2, red thread] Pick up an 8º, an 11º, an 8º, a square, two 11ºs, and an 8º, and sew through the two adjacent 11ºs in the previous stitch. Continue through the same hole of the square. Pick up an 8º.

Step 3

[Figure 2, blue thread] Attaching the last square in the group is a bit different since you already have the beginning two 11ºs. Pick up a new square, sew through the second two 11ºs added in step 1, pick up an 8º, and sew through the adjacent two 11ºs in the previous stitch. Continue on through the new square in the same direction.

Step 4

[Figure 3] Pick up an 8º, an 11º, and 8º, and sew through the next nine beads along the outer edge of the ring. Turn and sew through the open hole side of the square your thread is exiting. Snug your beads together. You are now in position to work the next section.

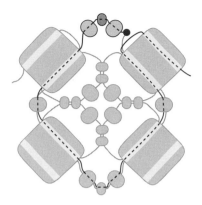

Figure 3

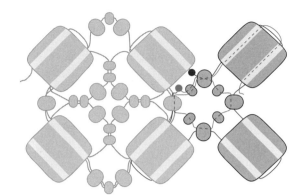

Figure 4

Step 5

[Figure 4, red thread] Pick up an 8º and a square, and sew through the open hole of the square. Repeat this stitch once, and then pick up an 8º, and sew through the nearest hole of the square added in step 2. Sew through the other hole of the same square and the 8º just above it to form a new cluster.

Step 6

[Figure 4, blue thread] Pick up an 11º, and sew through the next 8º in the inside ring. Repeat this stitch three times, and continue through the first 11º added in this step, the 8º, and the nearest hole of the adjacent square. Turn and sew through the other hole of the same square. Snug your beads together. You are now in position to work step 1. Repeat all the steps until you reach the desired length for your bracelet, ending and adding thread as needed.

Step 7

Attach a clasp to the ends. Use 11ºs to extend where needed to fit the clasp.

MATERIALS

7 in. (18cm) bracelet

34 squares

3g 8º seed beads

2g 11º seed beads

toggle clasp

3 yd. (2.7m) thread

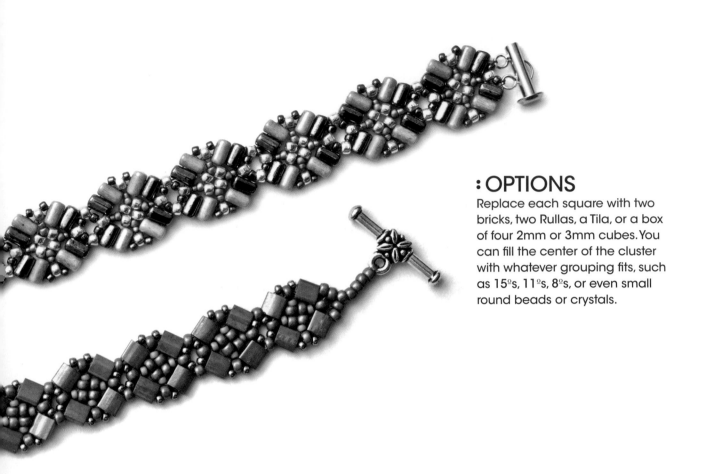

: OPTIONS

Replace each square with two bricks, two Rullas, a Tila, or a box of four 2mm or 3mm cubes. You can fill the center of the cluster with whatever grouping fits, such as 15°s, 11°s, 8°s, or even small round beads or crystals.

Note: Stop after a full section or a half section, but not in the middle of one. You may need to make the maximum number of sections you can fit in, and then lengthen to compensate by adding beads when attaching the clasp.

IMPORTANT TIPS

• Keep your thread on top of the work; don't let it wrap around behind the beads or other threads.

• When coming out of a square in the first cluster, sew through the corner 8°; when coming out of the center group, you sew directly into the next square.

• When making the inner grouping of the second cluster, be sure you catch just the 8°s and not the thread they are running on.

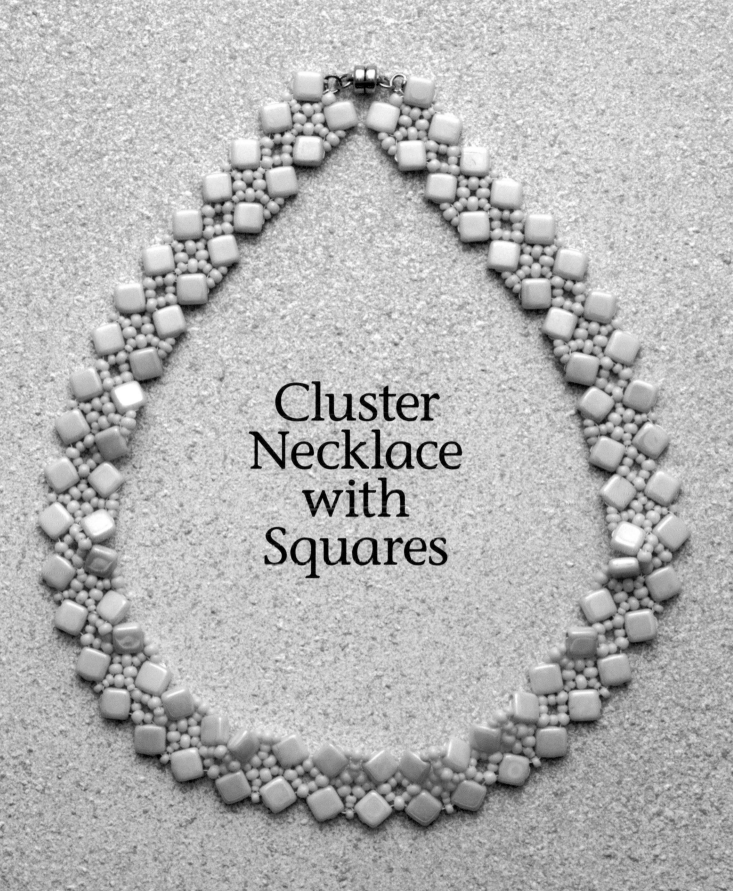

Cluster
Necklace
with
Squares

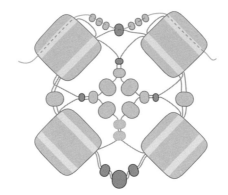

Figure

Note: To make a necklace instead of a bracelet, you will need to adjust a few things in the pattern to allow it to bend smoothly around the neck. The colored beads indicate where there are changes [Figure].

Follow the steps to create an "Advanced Cluster Bracelet with Squares" p. 95, with these changes:

Change 1

Along the top edge, add only an 11º seed bead instead of the grouping of an 8º seed bead, an 11º, and an 8º. This lets the top edge draw tighter than the bottom.

Change 2

Substitute a 15º seed bead in place of the 11º for the outer beads of the center grouping on the top and sides. This also helps the top draw tighter.

Optional Change 3

Substitute an 11º, an 8º, and an 11º along the bottom instead of an 8º, an 11º, and an 8º. This coordinates with the additional rows for the wider version.

Optional Change 4
[Figure, green thread, purple beads]

Using a separate thread, add a row at the top. Pick up three 15ºs on either side of the upper 11º. This also draws the necklace tighter at the top.

MATERIALS

16 in. (41cm) necklace

84 squares

4g 8º seed beads

5g 11º seed beads

magnetic clasp

3–4 yd. (2.7–3.7m) thread

Cluster Collar with Squares

Note: Add rows to the whole necklace or just to a section of the center front, as in this example. Either way, this necklace will get bolder and more dramatic with each new row you add, and you can stop at any point. If you have matching larger feature beads, you can add them along any outer row for a more dramatic look.

Step 1

Follow the steps to create a "Cluster Necklace with Squares," p. 99. For the first additional row: Exit the outside hole of a square along the lower edge. Pick up four 11º seed beads, an 8º seed bead, and four 11ºs. Sew through the next square and 8º, and continue through the following square. Repeat for the entire length of the necklace.

MATERIALS
7 in. (18cm) bracelet
84 squares
6g 8º seed beads
5g 11º seed beads
1g 15º seed beads
hook-and-loop clasp with
   jump rings
4 yd. (3.7m) thread

Figure 1

Figure 2

Note: Here, you are basically adding a new cluster, using the two lower squares as the new upper squares and adding two squares below.

Step 2

[Figure 1] For the second additional row: Exit the outside hole of the square your thread exited at the start of step 1, and continue through the four 11º's, the 8º, and three 11º's. Pick up a square, two 11º's, an 8º, and two 11º's, and sew through the new square again in the same direction.

Step 3

[Figure 2, blue thread] Pick up an 11º, an 8º, an 11º, a square, two 11º's, and an 8º, and sew through the first two 11º's added in the previous step. Continue

through the new square in the same direction.

Step 4

[Figure 2, purple thread] Sew through the adjacent 11º and the square above it as shown in figure 2. Pick up two 11º's and an 8º, and sew through the nearest two 11º's. Sew back through the square in the same direction and the center 8º. Continue through the adjacent square.

Step 5

[Figure 2, orange thread] Sew through the second two 11º's you picked up

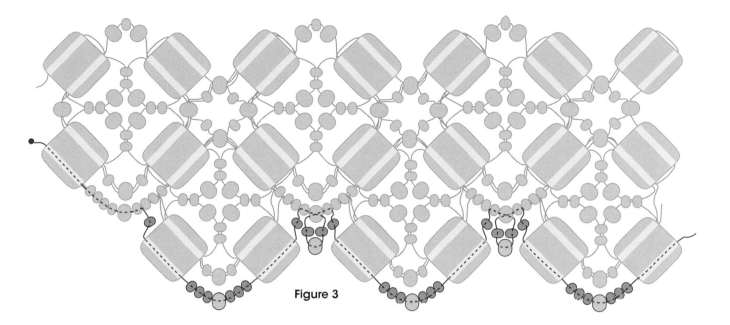

Figure 3

in step 2, pick up an 8º, and sew up through the first two 11ºs you picked up in step 4. Sew back through the square again, the nearest 11º, and the first new square added in this row. Continue through the next 11º, 8º, and 11º, and the adjacent square. Turn, and sew through the lower three 11ºs added in step 1, the 8º and the next three 11ºs. You are in position to continue the pattern as many times as desired.

Step 6

[Figure 3] For the third additional row: Exit one end square in the previous row. Continue through the four 11ºs, an 8º,

and an 11º. Pick up an 11º, and sew through the outside hole of the next square. Pick up three 11ºs, an 8º, and three 11ºs. Sew through the outside hole of the next square, pick up an 11º, and sew through the fourth 11º in the swag and the 8º. Pick up an 11º, an 8º, and an 11º, and sew back through the 8º in the same direction. Continue through the next 11º in the swag. Pick up an 11º and sew through the adjacent square. You are now in position to sew through the following swag and begin the pattern again. Attach a clasp half to each end of the necklace, and end the threads.

Note: Be careful that your additional rows do not pull the lower edge of the collar too tight. If necessary, add 11ºs or 15ºs to lengthen the swags.

Cluster Bracelet with Squares and SuperDuos

Note: This bracelet is basically the same design as the "Advanced Cluster Bracelet with Squares," but it incorporates SuperDuo beads instead of 8° seed beads.

Follow the steps to create an "Advanced Cluster Bracelet with Squares," p. 95, with the following changes:

Change 1

[Figure 1, blue SuperDuos] Pick up two SuperDuos in place of each top and bottom grouping of three 8° seed beads and one SuperDuo in place of each of the side 8°s.

Change 2

[Figure 1, red thread] Substitute SuperDuos in place of 8°s for the inner ring as shown in figure 1.

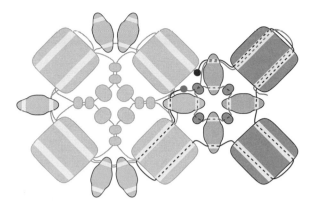

Figure 1

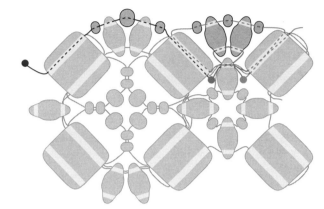

Figure 2

Change 3

[Figure 1, blue thread] Sew through the first SuperDuo again, pick up an 11º seed bead, and sew through the inner hole of the next SuperDuo. Repeat this stitch three times, sewing through the inner holes of all the center SuperDuos in sequence. Step up through the first 11º again, and continue through the upper hole of the next SuperDuo and the nearest hole of the adjacent square. You are now ready to start a new cluster.

Step 1

[Figure 2, darker beads, red thread] Begin the edging: With the thread exiting the outer hole of the square on the end of the bracelet, pick up an 11º, and sew through the corresponding hole of the next SuperDuo. Pick up an 8º, and sew through next SuperDuo. Pick up an 11º, and sew through the nearest hole of the next square.

Step 2

[Figure 2, darker beads, blue thread] Sew through the upper hole of the

adjacent SuperDuo. Pick up two SuperDuos, and sew back through the SuperDuo. Pull the SuperDuos to the work and place them.

Step 3

[Figure 2, darker beads, orange thread] Sew through the nearest hole of the next square. (Here you'll be going backward to the direction you are stitching.) Pick up an 11º, and sew through the open hole of the new SuperDuo, pick up an 11º, and sew through the following new SuperDuo. Pick up an 11º, and sew through the previous square, the SuperDuo, and the next square. From here, you can begin another pattern. Repeat along both sides. Add a clasp half to each end (see photo), and end the threads.

MATERIALS

7 in. (18cm) bracelet

32 squares

90 SuperDuos

1g 8º seed beads

2g 11º seed beads

toggle clasp

4 yd. (3.7m) thread

Double-Row Cluster Cuff

As in any right-angle weave stitch, each row will mesh with a new row. Widen any of these bracelets by turning back and building a row beneath the previous row. The clusters will alternate vertically as they do horizontally.

Step 1

[Figure 1, orange bead] Make a "Cluster Bracelet with Squares and SuperDuos," p. 104, but pick up only one SuperDuo along the edge where you are going to add a row.

Step 2

[Figure 1, red thread] Work your way through the beads so you are exiting the lower hole of the second square in the bottom of the previous secondary cluster in the previous row. Build a primary cluster on the bottom of the secondary cluster where you ended the first row.

Note: If you are only adding one row, remember to pick up two SuperDuos along the finishing edge [blue Super-Duos]. If you are going to add another row, pick up only one SuperDuo.

MATERIALS

7 in. (18cm) cuff

57 squares

132 SuperDuos

3g 8° seed beads

2g 11° seed beads

3-loop slide clasp

4 yd. (3.7m) thread

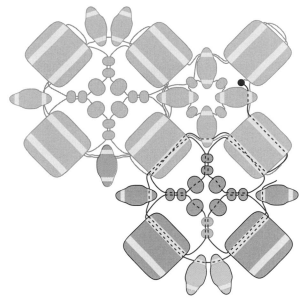

Figure 1

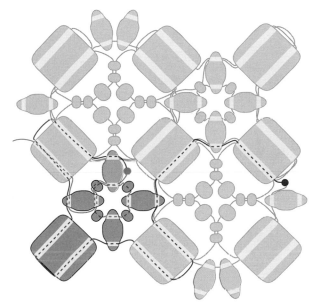

Figure 2

Step 3

[Figure 2, red and blue threads] Work your way through the beads so you are exiting the lower hole of the second square in the bottom of the previous secondary cluster in the previous row. Build a secondary cluster at the bottom of the primary cluster in the row above.

Step 4

Continue to build alternating clusters on the previous row until you have completed the desired length of the bracelet. Add edging as in the "Cluster Bracelet with Squares and SuperDuos."

Note: Two rows makes a 1⅛-in. (2.9cm) bracelet or narrow cuff, three rows makes a 1½-in. (3.8cm) cuff, and four rows makes a bold 2-in. (5cm) cuff.

: OPTIONS

This bracelet will handle any of the earlier substitutions, such as two bricks for each square, etc.

Cluster
Bracelet
with Bricks
and Studs

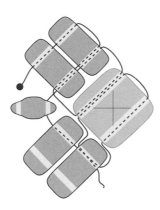

Figure 1

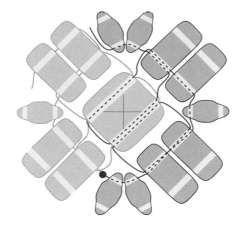

Figure 2

So far, we've changed some of the 8º seed beads to SuperDuos, and the squares to two bricks, Rullas, or Tilas—but the center grouping of 8ºs and 11º seed beads can be replaced, too. You will need a different technique to fit a two-hole center bead in place. Here is a fun piece that incorporates bricks and a small stud. Follow these changes in the basic process.

Step 1

[Figure 1] Work as in the "Cluster Bracelet with Squares and SuperDuos," p. 104, but replace each square with two bricks (or Rullas) throughout.

Step 2

[Figure 1, red thread] Replace the inner group of seed beads in the first cluster with a 7mm stud. First, attach the stud to the first two bricks. Pick up a SuperDuo and two bricks. Sew through the open hole of the stud, turn, and sew through the other hole of the stud. Skip the first brick, and sew through the following brick.

Step 3 [Figure 2, red thread] Pick up two SuperDuos and two bricks, and attach them to the nearest hole of the stud. With the thread exiting the two bricks, pick up a SuperDuo and two bricks, and sew down through the nearest hole of the stud. Turn, and sew back through the other hole of the stud. Skip the first brick, and sew through the second brick. Pick up two SuperDuos,

Step 3

Continue through the inner holes of the bricks and attach the bricks to the nearest SuperDuos around the stud as in the earlier versions of cluster stitch. With the thread exiting the upper right pair of bricks, turn, and sew through the open holes of the same two bricks. You are in position to continue building the bracelet by alternating between the secondary cluster, as in Figure 1, p. 105, and the primary cluster you just built. Finish by adding 11ºs and 8ºs along the edges besides the SuperDuos (see photo).

MATERIALS

7 in. (18cm) bracelet

64 bricks

8 small studs

62 SuperDuos

1g 8º seed beads

.5g 11º seed beads

toggle clasp

4 yd. (3.7m) thread

: OPTIONS

Use two Rullas or a square instead of two bricks. In the center, use a two-hole round the same size as the stud. Or double this row for a stunning cuff.

Cluster Gallery

Cluster Necklace with Drops: A slight adaptation makes room for the larger drops.

Cluster Necklace with Center: Group larger clusters for this necklace. The tops are embellished with piggy beads.

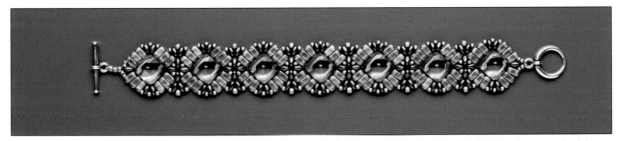

Cluster Bracelet with Large Stud: Work this piece like the small stud bracelet but add a third brick along each side.

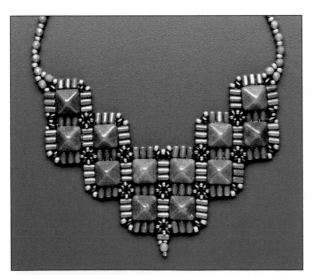

Cluster Necklace in Purple: This piece has large studs and triple Rullas.

Cluster Necklace in Pink: Rows of basic cluster stitch are joined into a real collar.

Acknowledgments

Thanks to Dianne and Erica at Kalmbach for their help and advice, and to all the Kalmbach staff who do such a great job of getting my books published and out to beaders all over the world. Thanks to my loving husband Rich, who beat the "Big C" this year with the bravest of attitudes and insisted I keep working on this book!

About the Author

Life is great on the western slope of Colorado. There is still no proper bead store here in Grand Junction—but a wonderful opportunity for an adventurous startup. Interest in beadwork is growing within our local Art Jewelers Guild, so I keep encouraging everyone to try new designs. The market is surviving the economic roller coaster so far. In the meantime, I work here somewhat isolated—not unlike many beaders out there—and try to keep up with the world through the web.

I'm always impressed with the wonderful beadwork going on all over the world and awed at the masterful workmanship of many exceptional beadwork designers. My Facebook friends keep me up-to-date on the latest trends and styles. Really, my favorite thing is to create a piece that I would love to wear myself. I appreciate the glamour and high art that I see in the magazines, but when I dress out here in the "wild" west, where everyone practically lives in jeans or shorts and tee shirts, I want something that fits, hangs right, and looks like it belongs. Much the same is true when I'm selling at a regional fair. I like designs that show the workmanship and explore the color possibilities, but don't overpower a simple top or a tee, or look odd on an arm that also lifts a bale of hay or goes trail biking on the weekend.

Sometimes I just don't look at what others have designed in case they are doing the same thing I am. Other times, I can't help myself from eagerly scouring the web, just to see whether anyone else is doing the same thing I am. I'm amazed when I find that my own designs are unique. Though there are bound to be similarities, since we are all working with the same beads and usually with the same stitches. Since it takes so long to get a book published the traditional way, an author's fear is that she will be beaten to the punch. So far, so good.

After spending the last year working on this book, I'm eager to get back to my own bead business. I've reworked my website and invite everyone to visit me there. I'm offering more for beaders—information, tips, free stuff, and brand-new designs. I'm increasing my gallery sales online as well. Visit me at virjenmettle.com.

What's in the future for me? I'm eager for some more artistic bead embroidery, yet I can't seem to get book writing out of my life. The process of writing a beadwork book is fun but also technical, stringent, and very different from the more artistic process that goes into making a creative design. Switching quickly between the two is difficult. I have to allot a long time for each kind of work it seems. A nice, long creative stretch looks appealing.

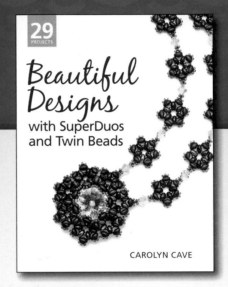
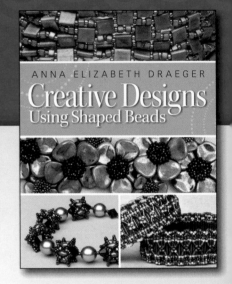